Love, Limits, and Consequences

Love, Limits, and Consequences

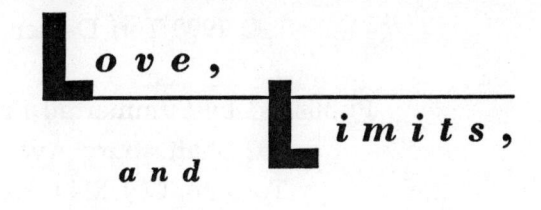

a positive, practical approach
to kids and discipline

**TERI DEGLER
and
YVONNE KASON,**
M.D.

SUMMERHILL PRESS, *Toronto*

© 1990 Teri Degler

Published by Summerhill Press Ltd.
52 Shaftesbury Ave.,
Toronto, ON M4T 1A2

Distributed by University of Toronto Press
5201 Dufferin Street,
Downsview, ON M3H 5T8

Cover design by Linda Gustafson Design
Text design by JAQ

Printed and bound in the United States

Canadian Cataloguing in Publication Data
Degler, Teri, 1948-
Love, limits and consequences : a positive,
practical approach to kids and discipline
Includes bibliographical references.
ISBN 0-929091-12-4
1. Discipline of children. 2. Child rearing.
I. Kason, Yvonne, 1953-   . II. Title.

HQ770.4.D44 1990   649'.64   C90-093656-8

The names of children, parents, and teachers in this book have been changed and bear no resemblance to their actual identity.

*For Jason, Valerie, and Veronica,
and all the other children who brighten our lives.*

ACKNOWLEDGEMENTS

We would like to express our thanks to everyone who helped us — in such a variety of creative ways — with the preparation of this book, especially, Dale Pond, Dr. Ruth Brooks, Dr. Marcia Landau, Lawrie Rotenberg, Joe Trivers, Michael and Jane Gauthier, and Suzanne Sherkin. We would also like to thank Patti Kirk and Bill Elleker from Parent Books in Toronto for their help with the "Guide to Books on Parenting."

Contents

Introduction — 9

PART ONE: Balancing love and limits

Chapter One
COMBINING LOVE AND LIMITS — 17

Chapter Two
KIDS LIKE TO KNOW WHERE THEY STAND — 28

Chapter Three
SETTING CONSEQUENCES AND FOLLOWING THROUGH — 44

Chapter Four
FACING THE CONSEQUENCES — 63

Chapter Five
A THEORY OF HOPE — 90

Chapter Six
WHAT TO DO WHEN DON'T DOESN'T WORK — 106

Chapter Seven
LOVE NEVER SPOILED A CHILD — 131

Chapter Eight
POSSESSIVENESS IS NOT LOVE — 144

Chapter Nine
I'LL NEVER DO THAT WHEN I GROW UP — 154

Chapter Ten
TROUBLESHOOTING 165

Chapter Eleven
IT'S ALL RIGHT TO CRY 179

PART TWO: **Special problems, special solutions**
Chapter Twelve
THE NOT SO TERRIBLE TWOS 199

Chapter Thirteen
SCHOOL BLUES 207

Chapter Fourteen
HALF A FAMILY — A WHOLE CHILD 223

Chapter Fifteen
SLOW CHILD IN A FAST WORLD 236

Chapter Sixteen
THE WHIRLWIND CHILD 247

Chapter Seventeen
MICKEY: A DISTURBED CHILD AND THE POWER OF LOVE 261

Chapter Eighteen
CONCLUSION: HUG ME, HOLD ME, TELL ME I'M GOOD 268

PART THREE: **Further reading**
Chapter Nineteen
A GUIDE TO BOOKS ON PARENTING 281

Index 303

Introduction

Love, Limits, and Consequences is a book for parents, teachers, day-care workers and anyone who spends much time with children. It deals with positive methods of handling everyday discipline problems and, more importantly, tells how to prevent them. The book stresses a child's need for unconditional love, physical affection and attention. But it also emphasizes the importance of setting boundaries around a child's behavior. The purpose of *Love, Limits, and Consequences* is to show how a loving, expressive atmosphere can be created within the framework of a secure, structured environment.

The book is divided into three sections. The first section, "Balancing Love and Limits," examines the most essential elements in what we call positive parenting and teaching. This information is broken down into ten simple guidelines that can be used by any parent or teacher to improve his relationships with children and to handle specific behavior problems. In the second section, "Special Problems, Special Solutions," we take a look at some of the most common problems faced by parents today, such as raising a child in a single-parent home, coping with poor school performance and understanding a child with special needs. The third section, "A Guide to Books on Parenting," is intended to help you make sense of the welter of information on child development and parenting available today.

Love, Limits, and Consequences is the result of a collaboration between Yvonne Kason Hintermeister, a mother and medical doctor, and me, Teri Degler, a teacher and writer. Dr. Kason, a specialist in family medicine for the past eleven years, has had a great deal of experience with children in the home and in her practice. She is an assistant professor in the Department of Family and Community Medicine at the University of Toronto, where she teaches family medicine to students and residents. As part of her busy medical practice, Dr. Kason does extensive family counseling and psychotherapy. She has a Master of Education degree in applied psychology and has written a number of articles for medical journals.

My background is in special education. I have a Master of Arts degree from the University of New Mexico. There I worked with children with emotional problems, and I studied both educational methods and therapeutic techniques. Since then, I have taught in France, Austria, and Canada. I have worked with all types of children — from those who would be called "normal" to those with severe disturbances such as schizophrenia. But much of my work has been with children who had behavior and discipline problems they could learn to overcome. I've been writing about children with such problems — and about how parents and teachers could help them — for years. When I thought about putting the concepts I had been writing about into a book, I decided I'd like to have the input of a doctor and a parent. I was delighted when Dr. Kason agreed to collaborate with me on the project, because she has had so much experience with children.

One point about language: the feminist movement has made us aware that it is not acceptable to always use the pronoun "he" for a child or person whose sex has not been specified. A solution to the problem is to use "he/she." We find this awkward. So when we are referring to a child in general, rather than one whose sex is known, we use he and she in alternate chapters. In chapters where the child is a "she" the parent or teacher is a "he," and vice versa. (Today, fathers often take as active a role in child rearing as mothers do.)

When I first approached Dr. Kason about working with me on a book she told me she was particularly excited about the idea because she had been unable to find exactly the kind of straightforward, practical book on discipline she wanted to give to parents who were having trouble handling their children's behavior problems. Many parents were having difficulty because they thought discipline meant spanking. Most of those who believed spanking was acceptable used it as their only disciplinary measure. Eventually many of them discovered that spanking didn't improve their children's long-term behavior or that it had detrimental effects. Parents who did not think spanking was acceptable, simply didn't use it. When behavior problems occurred, these parents usually tried to reason with their kids. But when that didn't work, they had no disciplinary measure to fall back on. In *Love, Limits, and Consequences* we show you that there are plenty of alternatives to spanking. The disciplinary techniques we discuss are not only more effective than spanking, they also leave your children's self-respect — and their respect for you — intact.

The ten guidelines in *Love, Limits, and Consequences* will help you develop positive parenting or teaching habits without making you feel that you have to drastically alter your personality or adopt ideas that are foreign to you. This is important, because how you relate to kids depends a lot on who you are. Dr. Kason and I doubt that people with natural leanings toward using fairly strict discipline or toward allowing children tremendous freedom are going to change overnight because they read a book in which an expert tells them they should.

Yet many people attempt to do just that. They read a fairly good book or an article about a particular way of dealing with children, and with great enthusiasm they begin to try the idea out on their kids. But they are not able to stick with it, so eventually the attempt fails. Then they try something else — or they flounder because they can't decide exactly which approach is right. They are strict one day, then they feel guilty and loosen all restrictions the next. They've heard it is best to reason with a child, so they reason until they are completely exasperated, then they yell. Or they let a discipline situation get so out of control that *they* lose control.

It's clear that no parent wants to raise children this way. But it is almost impossible for parents to be consistent if they are trying to apply techniques or ideas they are not comfortable with. This is why we provide you with guidelines rather than dogmatic rules. Although you may discover that you do have to change some of your habits if you want to be a more effective parent or teacher, you should still be comfortable with most of the information we give and find it adaptable to your own personality and parenting style.

Part One

Balancing love and limits

Chapter One

Combining love and limits

This book contains ten guidelines that show you how to combine love and discipline in raising and working with children. These guidelines are easy to understand, easy to apply, and practical.

Everyone agrees that children need to be loved. But love is a very general term, and it means different things to different people. In this book, we talk about the specific ways you can show your children that you love them — and at the same time build their confidence and self-esteem. When parents or teachers use our ten guidelines, they start to build a framework for positive discipline. One of the best things about these guidelines is that they allow for differences in personalities and tolerance levels. They can be used by people who tend to be fairly lenient with their children and by those who only feel comfortable with a structured environment. They also leave room for adults to rely on their intuition and common sense — and to choose methods that take children's individual differences into account, too.

Almost all the popular books on child rearing available today are written from the point of view of a particular psychological theory. In promoting their theory, the authors generally concentrate on making the theory fit the entire process of child rearing. The problem with this, as Dr. Kason and I see it, is that the authors sometimes get so caught up in their theory they miss the opportunity to look at other effective methods.

Dr. Kason and I take an approach that represents a combination of ideas. Instead of promoting any one theory, we focus on the methods we have seen work time and again over the years. These methods are reflected in our ten guidelines. Together the guidelines represent the most important elements in your overall approach to children. When you get into the habit of using the guidelines, you'll get into the habit of positive parenting or teaching. You'll know how to respond in specific, positive ways to your children; you'll be able to eliminate the need for a great deal of discipline, yet you'll be able, when it's necessary, to discipline in a way that keeps a child's self-esteem intact and assures him that his world is a secure, trustworthy place.

From the time Dr. Kason first specialized in family medicine, she had been looking for a book on child rearing that emphasized the importance of both unconditional love and reasonable, appropriate limits, and that provided parents with a number of simple, effective alternatives to shouting and spanking. When I first started working in the United States in a special clinic and school for children with behavior problems, an event occurred that also made me see the need for such a book. One afternoon when a mother came to pick up her daughter she asked me if she could talk to me. Her daughter had been at the clinic for about six months and had made tremendous progress. The mother said, "You know, I can see how much Tina has improved since coming to this clinic. But there is still a huge difference in how she acts here and how she acts at home. She seems to behave so well and to be so much more cooperative here. But when she's at home I still can't get her to cooperate with me. What do you do here, anyway? How can I learn to relate to her like that?"

"Well," I said, "it's easy. You just..." And I stopped. I realized I couldn't describe the process. I knew it was simple, but I didn't know how to explain it. I told Tina's mother I'd get her a book on the subject. But when I looked for a book that summed things up, I couldn't find one.

I started going through the many texts on child psychology I had studied, and although I found one effective technique here and another there, no one book contained all the techniques I thought were essential or put them together in a way that would make it easy for Tina's mother to apply them.

I began to observe the people I worked with even more closely. I became increasingly certain that the most effective parents, teachers, and day-care workers shared certain methods of dealing with children. It didn't seem to matter whether they were highly trained professionals or simple, loving parents with a good deal of common sense. Nor did it matter if they tended to be permissive or strict, as long as they were not given to extremes. If they were professionals, it didn't matter which particular psychological theory they had been trained in. What did matter was that all these people loved children, respected them as human beings, and knew how to show this love and respect in concrete ways. They also knew how to structure an environment so that there wouldn't be a need for too much discipline. But they were capable of using discipline, when it was needed, in a reasonable and appropriate way. Eventually I realized that the most essential aspects of this positive approach could be boiled down into ten guidelines.

Over the years, Dr. Kason and I have known many parents and teachers who used these guidelines. One of them was Marsha, a teacher and mother I worked with in Albuquerque, New Mexico. She typifies what Dr. Kason and I think of as the parent or teacher with a positive approach. The following is a description of the way Marsha dealt with children on a daily basis. Later, when you read about the ten guidelines, you'll see that each one is covered in the way Marsha related to her own children and the ones she taught. This doesn't mean Marsha was perfect. She sometimes lost her temper, cried in frustration, yelled at her kids, felt inadequate, and fell far short of her expectations for herself. Still, she worked at using the guidelines and, because she could adapt them to her own personality and tolerance levels, she could apply them fairly consistently.

One of the first things I noticed about Marsha was that she always let kids know exactly where they stood with her. She told them clearly what their limits were, so the children knew exactly what they were and were not allowed to do. Since their limits were clearly defined, the children didn't need to test Marsha by misbehaving repeatedly or by escalating their annoying types of behavior until she lost her temper with them.

The kids were confident that Marsha said what she meant and meant what she said. She always explained what the consequence — a concept often used to replace the idea of punishment — of any misbehavior would be. The kids knew that if they misbehaved, Marsha would be sure to follow through with the consequence she had set down. If she told a student she would take away his squirt gun if he used it, she *would* take it away. But the consequences she used were always fair, reasonable, and appropriate.

Marsha once told me she had discovered early on that kids needed a lot less discipline when their basic needs were being met. Since a child's need for love and attention is as great as his need for food and shelter, she and her husband made sure their kids received a lot of physical affection and praise in the home. In the classroom, she took time to emphasize each child's accomplishments and to use praise in a way that helped the child improve and that developed his self-esteem. She focused her attention on positive behavior rather than negative and on a child's strengths instead of his weaknesses. When she was displeased with a child's actions she made it clear that it was the misbehavior she didn't approve of, not the child himself. She would say, "Hitting is not acceptable!" "Shoving your sister hurts her. It's not allowed." "It makes me angry when you grab things out of my hand!" But I never heard her say, "You're a bad girl," or, "You are a terrible boy for hitting." Even when she had to tell a child she didn't like what he was doing, the child was confident that she still liked him, accepted him, and regarded him with warmth and respect. Marsha didn't put conditions on her love.

But she did sometimes have to struggle to overcome a tendency to be overprotective. The fact that she was a bit of a "mother hen" didn't please her; she often had to make a real effort not to step in every time she saw a child having difficulty accomplishing something. Still, she made the effort because she realized that children need room to try things out for themselves and make their own mistakes. At home and in the classroom, Marsha tried to encourage children to express their emotions honestly and openly. The children had plenty of opportunity to play loudly, get dirty, experiment and be messy.

Encouraging children to express themselves was not something that came easy for Marsha. She had been raised in an extremely repressive environment by a father who believed that everything had to be done perfectly and that children should be seen and not heard. When Marsha became a mother she was determined to raise her children differently, but as time went on she discovered that she often automatically treated children the way her father had treated her. Shocked by this, she enrolled in a parenting course where she learned that most parents tend to raise their kids much the way they were raised. She also learned how to replace the ingrained, negative responses she had absorbed from her parents with more positive ones.

One of Marsha's strongest qualities was her ability to prevent trouble before it began. She was tuned in to the children's moods and on the lookout for possible problems. This enabled her to diffuse many situations that might have become explosive. At home and in school, she also looked for ways to structure the environment so that the need for discipline was minimized.

One reason the positive approach — used by Marsha and many other parents and teachers — is so successful is that it takes into account a child's tremendous need for love and attention. Children who don't get enough loving attention will often misbehave in order to get any kind of attention — even if it is negative. A child who is starved for affection can actually find being punished preferable to being ignored. The most effective parents and teachers know the importance of unconditional love; there are no strings attached to the love the parents give the children or to the warm regard the teachers feel for their students. The children are accepted — and they know it.

Each of our ten guidelines is individually important. But unless they are put together and used as part of an overall framework for positive parenting and teaching, they won't be as effective. Let's look, for example, at the guideline that relates to giving kids enough attention. Once I was tutoring a boy, Jake, who was getting into a lot of trouble at home. When his mother, Elizabeth, mentioned the problem to me, I told her that one of the first things she needed to do was to make sure the boy was getting enough attention and affection. The mother interrupted me. She said she was absolutely certain there was no relationship between the amount of attention Jake received and his behavior problems. When I asked why, she explained that she had read an article on the subject of attention in a parenting magazine. After reading the article, Elizabeth had admitted to herself that her son probably needed more attention. She was interested in the article's claim that giving attention to a child who needs it can sometimes greatly improve his behavior. Since Jake had been getting into quite a bit of trouble, she decided she was going to make a sincere effort to give him more attention, especially in the ways the article recommended. But after several weeks, Jake's behavior hadn't improved at all. Eventually, she stopped making any effort to give him more attention. Elizabeth concluded that giving a child attention — even one like Jake who needed it — could do nothing to improve behavior.

But the real reason Jake's behavior didn't improve was that Elizabeth wasn't using other essential guidelines in her approach to Jake. She did not, for instance, discipline Jake when he misbehaved. Jake told me, "Oh, she always says she's going to discipline me — but she never does. Last week when I got in trouble at school, she told me I was grounded for the weekend. But on Saturday night all I had to do was plead with her a little and she let me go out. I knew she would. She never sticks to anything she says."

It's easy to see how Elizabeth's repeated inability to follow through with the discipline she said she was going to carry out undermined her efforts to give her son attention. She would give Jake attention verbally, praise him or make encouraging comments, but her words had no real meaning for Jake. He knew, from experience, that his mother often didn't mean the things she said. The fact that she was saying something he wanted to hear was not reason enough to start believing her.

Experiences like the one with Jake and Elizabeth have made both Dr. Kason and myself feel strongly about the importance of including all the essential guidelines in one book. In the following chapters we discuss each of the ten guidelines in detail. We've kept the information as simple and straightforward as possible, and we've provided many examples so that parents, teachers, and daycare workers will find the guidelines easy to apply. Of course, applying the guidelines isn't automatically easy. Sometimes using the guidelines requires self-examination and honesty. Often it means you have to make repeated efforts until a certain response becomes second nature for you. But, ultimately, you will reap the benefits of a more positive relationship with your kids. You'll also be armed with a number of specific techniques for improving children's behavior, and you'll have some concrete ideas about how to combine discipline and love.

Before we go on to the first of our ten guidelines, we want to discuss the subject of parental guilt. It is our belief that a parent is not necessarily to blame when a child develops behavior problems or has difficulty adjusting. There are still psychiatrists and psychologists who tend to lay much of the blame for a child's emotional problems at the feet of the parents, but most mental health professionals today believe that many factors — such as heredity, brain chemistry and birth order — may contribute to the development of behavioral and emotional problems in children. Every child has his own makeup, his own personality. And every child responds differently to the things people say and do to him.

In our work, Dr. Kason and I have come across children with behavior problems whose parents have had adequate parenting skills and sincere love for their children. The question of why a particular child is troubled — or gets into trouble — cannot be answered simplistically. There is too much that science does not yet understand about personality and the workings of the human mind.

Even though we sometimes discuss parenting habits that we feel can have negative effects, we want to make it clear that we are not trying to make parents feel guilty or blame them for everything that goes wrong with their kids. There are too many factors, too many variables, too many unknowns. While there can never be any guarantees in a field as complex and little understood as human behavior, we believe the positive parenting framework we discuss in this book can contribute greatly to a child's general emotional health and happiness.

Chapter Two

Kids like to know where they stand

Kids like to know where they stand. If they don't know, they will test you until they find out. You've all seen children when they are testing — getting louder and louder, playing rougher and rougher, reaching nearer and nearer to an object they think might be forbidden — until, finally, someone yells, "All right now, that's *enough!*"

When you set clear limits, you tell children where they stand, so they don't have to guess about what they may or may not do. Limits do not have to be negative. And, though they are restrictions, they do not have to be totally restrictive. For instance, when you tell a child she is allowed to play in the backyard but not allowed to leave it, you have set a clear limit. But the child is not overly restricted. There are still wonderful things to do in the yard: she can swing, play in the sandbox, make mud pies, build a fort, play with the dog or climb a tree that's safe.

Many of us don't like to put restrictions on children. We are afraid the setting of limits might thwart their creativity, dampen their curiosity, make them become rigid in their attitudes and thought, or keep them from reaching their potential. We are also afraid they won't like the restrictions or won't like us because we have laid them down.

In all our years of working with children, Dr. Kason and I have never met a child who was not more comfortable with having limits set for her than with not knowing where she stood. Of course, the limits had to be appropriate, reasonable, and just — and they had to be set down in a way that showed respect for the child and her abilities.

At the opposite end of the spectrum from those parents and teachers who do not feel comfortable with restrictions are those who feel the need for rules that cover absolutely everything a child might want to do or even think about doing. This is not necessary, either, and can be harmful.

Regardless of which side of the spectrum they fall on — as long as they are not given to extremes — parents, teachers, and child-care workers can learn to use limit setting as a technique that provides children with a structure to let them know what they can and cannot do and still give them freedom. A loving, supportive environment doesn't have to be one where there are no ground rules or where children never learn the consequences of their behavior. In fact, our experience shows that kids are at their creative, curious, expressive best when firm — but appropriate — boundaries are placed around their behavior.

It reminds me of the young horses who kicked and frolicked in the fenced-in pasture behind our house when I was a child. Even though they looked happy, I believed that they couldn't be *really* happy unless they were allowed to run free. I could imagine them, wild and unrestrained, galloping joyously across the desert with the wind lifting their manes and tails. When one colt did accidentally break out, however, he was frantic, dashing this way and that, frightened by cars on the highway, running from barking dogs, and catching his hooves in the holes left by burrowing animals. He was happy to be found and brought back into the pasture, where he was sure and safe.

Two types of limits

Limits are the boundaries we set around a child's behavior, much as a fence is set around a pasture. There are two kinds of limits: those dealing with safety and those dealing with behavior. Safety limits are set when we tell a child not to play in the road, touch a hot stove, put a pin in an electric outlet, or play with stray dogs. Behavior limits are set when we tell a child how much noise and mess she can make, how she must treat other people and, where she can play. Sometimes safety and behavior limits overlap. For example, you might tell a child she is not allowed to play in the neighbor's backyard because it's full of things that might be dangerous, or because it's not polite to play in someone else's backyard without asking permission.

Limits and safety

In general, safety limits are much easier to set than behavior limits. One reason for this is that safety limits deal with the fairly concrete and easily defined issue of what will or will not harm a child. Most adults are aware of the dangers that exist in a child's environment and have little difficulty warning a child about them. The most effective safety limits are stated in a calm voice and in words you are quite sure the child understands.

Setting limits for safety can never be as effective as providing a safe environment. One of the reasons for this is that a number of potentially dangerous activities — chewing, poking, reaching, pulling and climbing — are "tasks" that are related to stages of learning and development. When a child is in a particular stage she has a powerful inner urge to master all the tasks associated with that stage. For example, when a fifteen-month-old child is trying to learn to climb, she will attempt — again and again — to climb every chair, table and staircase she sets her eyes on. Trying to keep her from climbing at this stage would be extremely difficult; it would also keep her from mastering the task. The alternative is to provide her with plenty of safe, supervised opportunities for climbing and to make her environment as free as possible from things she could get hurt climbing on.

At certain stages, children are going to put everything they can get their hands on into their mouths, and they are going to chew on and possibly swallow these things. At one stage they might take an electric cord and bite on it, at another they might tug on it till a lamp topples onto them. When they find something like a bobby pin, they will try to stick it in a hole, like an electric outlet. It's our responsibility as adults to realize how strong these urges to explore and experiment are and to keep potentially dangerous things out of our children's reach. It is also necessary that we make sure our children have plenty of opportunity to practice the tasks that are so important to their learning and development. A fifteen-month-old who starts climbing five minutes after you have told her to stop is not being "bad"; she is simply following an inner desire to master an essential life skill. The best way to keep from getting frustrated with her is to provide her with a good place to climb.

Limits and behavior

There are more variables involved in setting behavior limits than there are in setting safety limits, and this sometimes makes them more difficult to set. Also, some behavior limits change with circumstances. For example, if your child wants to pound on a particularly noisy drum some well-meaning uncle gave her for Christmas, there are a variety of limits you might set. You might say, "You can play the drum all you want, but you have to play it in the rec room or go outside with it, you can't play it in here because the baby's sleeping." Or, "Of course you can play the drum, but we'll have to limit it to fifteen minutes, I've got a headache today and I don't think I can take more than that." Or, "I'm sorry but you just can't play the drum today, Grandma's sick and it's snowing too hard for you to take it outside. You could play with your wooden peg set if you feel like pounding, or you could play a record if you want music."

Setting limits in advance

Anytime a child begins — or asks permission to begin — an activity that you feel is going to need a limit, you have to make your expectations clear immediately. As soon as your four-year-old daughter picks up a toy you know your three-year-old son is going to want desperately when he wakes up from his nap, you might say, "I am sure Andy wouldn't mind if you played with his toy for awhile, but I know he's really going to want it when he wakes up. It won't be long before he's up. You can play with his toy for fifteen minutes. Then you'll need to pick another toy. I'll remind you before the time is up."

Setting limits in advance lets children know what is expected of them, so they don't have to keep testing you to find out. And, in the case of time limits, it helps prevent the hassle that sometimes goes along with bringing an end to a pleasurable activity. When I take my goddaughters, ages five and six, swimming, I tell them exactly how long we are going to be able to stay in the water, and I point out the time passing on the clock on the wall. The one time I forgot to set a time limit in advance and explain it to them, they both burst into tears when I said, "Okay, it's time to go."

Some limits are more standard than the examples given above; they don't change with circumstances, and so they don't really need to be set in advance. For instance, a young child is told she can play in the backyard, but not leave it; an older child that she can play anywhere on the block, but not cross any streets; a still older child is allowed to ride her bike as far as the park, but no farther. Even though these limits remain standard for a period of time, with some children they may need to be reinforced often.

Limits you can live with

Many adults are more reluctant to set behavior limits than safety limits. Since a child can be hurt if she breaks a safety limit, we don't feel guilty about laying down the law and sticking to it. But with behavior limits our own wants, personal preferences, and tolerance levels are often involved. Many modern parents and teachers have the idea they should ignore their own wants and needs for the sake of the child's self-expression. In reality it is essential that we strike a balance between the two.

Most behavior limits depend on a balance between your tolerance level, the tolerance levels of the other people around, and the child's need for self-expression. A child needs to develop cleanliness, politeness and respect for property. She also needs room to get dirty, make a mess, explore, and vent her anger. Sometimes you need for her to be quiet; sometimes she needs to make noise.

After weighing safety factors, determine how much noise or mess you can tolerate and set the limits at that particular level in advance. Limits that don't take your own tolerance levels into account are doomed to failure. If you cannot bear the sound of drumming but tell your child she can pound on her drum all she wants, then try to ignore the drumming once it has started, you will almost invariably reach a point where you can no longer endure the irritation. Then you'll explode and yell at the child to stop. This has three negative effects. You feel terrible because you've yelled at the child; the child is scared and confused because she had no warning that she was doing anything wrong; and it does nothing to improve her future behavior because she has no concrete way of knowing exactly what made you so angry. Next time, she will wonder what it is that she is *not* supposed to do. Should she not play the drum so loud? Should she not play it so long? Should she not play it at all? She doesn't know, so she'll try to discover the answer by testing. She will grab the drum time and again and pound on it until she gets screamed at. This is not a child who is "bad," this is a child who is simply, and quite naturally, trying to find out where she stands.

There is nothing wrong with you if you are the kind of person who needs a lot of peace, order and quiet in your life. If you are, you are probably going to set behavior limits that are somewhat more restrictive than those set by someone who doesn't mind noise and disruption. There is nothing wrong with that, if your limits are reasonable and if you take into consideration the child's needs to explore and express herself. You'll still need to find a time when she can bang a drum to her heart's content and a place where she can make all the mess she wants. If you don't, your disciplinary measures will eventually fail. A child who is excessively restricted will usually lose her spirit or rebel. She may not begin to fight back until she's older. But in most cases, the human spirit refuses to be completely restrained for long.

Limits that fit the child

Just as the needs and tolerance levels of adults vary, so do those of children. This is often true of children within the same family. Obviously, age makes a big difference. Young children need specific safety limits. As they grow older some safety limits will be lifted, while expectations regarding behavior are increased. A little child can only ride her trike in the driveway, an older child can ride her bike to school; a two-year-old will fling her food sometimes, while a four-year-old can be expected to have some table manners. Unfortunately, some parents forget to revise limits as their child matures: I know of an eight-year-old girl who lives in a small, safe country town who is not allowed to ride her bike off the driveway.

Age is not the only factor to consider when setting limits. Some children need more structure than others. Some can be trusted to use their own judgment about what might be dangerous; others cannot.

Some children need to be messier a[nd...]
others. There are also children who[, for legiti-]
mate reasons, have a tremendous [need]
to express. Some children are so c[autious the slight-]
est word of warning keeps them out o[f trouble...]
need to have warnings fired off like flare gun[s at]
regular intervals. To set appropriate limits for your
children, you have to observe carefully and be sensitive to their differences. No one can tell you exactly
where to set limits for any particular child; you have
to do it yourself. And limits are effective only when
they are appropriate.

Different limits for siblings

Children with different personalities within the same
family can be given their own sets of limits and still
handled fairly, if parents are sensitive enough. This
is often made easier by the fact that the children are
not the same age, and consequently expect to be
treated differently. Explaining your reasoning helps,
too. For instance, you can say, "Billy, the reason we
let Sarah go to the swimming pool with her friends,
when we only let you go with one of us — even
though you're older — is that she took her swimming lessons last year when you didn't want to go."
(You might add that you really hope he'll take lessons in July so he can go to the pool on his own by
August, but you should probably avoid a heated
lecture on how you told him he'd be sorry if he didn't
take those lessons!)

Of course, allowing for differences is one thing,
and playing favorites is another. In general, after we

w for differences in age, we need to try to make
e standards for all the children in one family as
consistent as possible.

Other hints on setting limits

Be positive when you are setting limits. Even when you are setting down restrictions you can emphasize what the child *can* do. For instance, when a child asks if she can go to the park alone and you are not going to allow it you can say, "I'm sorry but you can't go to the park by yourself, you're still too young for that. But you can go with me, and I'll be able to take you about four o'clock."

Another good way to make limits more effective is to offer alternatives and let the child choose between them. For example, "Baseballs are for throwing outside, Sarah. If you want to throw the baseball you'll have to go outside. Do you want to do that? Or do you want to stay here and play quietly?" Or, if you have a Nerf ball you might say, "Do you want to take the baseball outside and throw it or do you want to throw the Nerf ball in here?" In Chapter Six, we talk more about offering alternatives.

Time limits can also be effective and often provide a workable compromise between what your child wants and what you can tolerate. When you are getting worn out at the park, for instance, you can let your child know it will soon be time to go by saying, "You can swing for five more minutes, Billy, and then we'll have to go." This also works with numbers: "You can go down the slide three more times, then we are going home." Time and number limits, however, often don't work well unless the child gets reminders along the way. For instance, Billy's parent would need to say, "You've got two minutes left now," and then, "Time's almost up," then "Time's up." If you're a teacher and you've told your class they can have "free time" for half an hour, you'll need to warn them when twenty minutes are up, then again when twenty-five minutes have passed. With number limits, you can count along with young children to help them understand.

When setting limits, remember to use words the child understands. It is very easy to forget that a toddler might not have a clue what the word "dangerous" means, or that a three- or four-year-old, who knows perfectly well what "hot" means, might not yet understand the word "boiling."

Your tone of voice is also important. When setting safety limits, you want to make a child understand the danger, but you don't want to terrify her. I took my dog along once when visiting a friend. When her three children, aged six to two, saw my large but gentle dog come into the house, they ran to their mother, hid behind her and began to tremble uncontrollably and sob. I was surprised by the extreme reaction, and I asked my friend why they were so afraid. She replied that there was a dog on their street she didn't trust so she'd told them not to play with dogs. Those may have been the words she used to explain the situation to her children, but something in her voice must have conveyed a much more terrifying message.

Alternatives to setting limits

Probably the most surefire way to keep limits effective is to use as few of them as possible. Setting limits is not the only means of preventing misbehavior or encouraging good behavior. If you can provide your children with an environment that is safe, you'll have much less need to tell them what they cannot do. When the first child comes along, a home sometimes needs quite a bit of modifying before it's child-proof. Things you don't want to have damaged or that are potentially dangerous have to be removed or kept out of reach. Of course, the rest of the world hasn't been child-proofed, and sometimes you may not be able to fully child-proof your own home. This is especially true when you have both a baby and preschoolers. The older children can't be deprived of all their toys, for instance, just because the toys are not suitable for younger children. You must set careful limits and keep on top of who's playing with what.

Other alternatives to setting limits include asking the child not to do something. We can explain our expectations; we can reason, and we can provide her with a good behavior model by the way we act ourselves. These ideas are discussed more thoroughly in Chapter Six.

Be reasonably consistent

Limits, to be effective, need to be reasonably consistent. It makes sense that a child is going to find it easier to stay within boundaries she is accustomed to. It is, of course, impossible to be perfectly consistent. Circumstances are always changing, special occasions do exist, and there are exceptions to every rule. It is not even desirable to strive for absolute consistency. We want our kids to learn to think for themselves and to make judgments. We also have to be able to admit freely that we are sometimes wrong: to stick to a limit even though we know the limit was a mistake, for the sake of consistency, is a far worse mistake.

In general, it's important to strive to be *reasonably* consistent with behavior limits, and when you're not consistent, try to explain why things are different from one day to the next. It's perfectly reasonable, for instance, to let a child stay up to watch a television special that's on late because of a time-zone difference, to have two pieces of cake on her birthday, to spray her hair green for Halloween, or to stay out late for a concert when her favorite band comes to town. As long as it's understood that it's a special occasion, there is usually no problem — except that we often need to reaffirm the normal limits once, so to speak, the party's over.

Safety limits are somewhat different. They need to be kept as consistent as possible. It is often better to make safety limits with exceptions than it is to make absolutely inflexible limits. For example, instead of making the rule, "Never play with dogs," you set a limit such as "You must always ask me before you go up to a dog you don't know."

You have to be consistent with children is a saying that is popular but controversial. Some parenting experts say you do not need to worry at all about consistency, that it is not a significant issue. One reason for the disagreement on the subject seems to be that few people are clear about what *consistency* means — or when it should be applied. Consistency means setting sensible standards and keeping them the same as long is it is reasonable to do so. But being flexible is also important. And, of course, no parent or teacher is perfectly consistent. There are times when tempers are short, when we cannot stand as much dirt and mess as we could the day before, when we have headaches or are under stress or are having a bad day. We all fall short of our ideals for behaving consistently with children. That's okay, especially if we are open enough to tell our children what's going on and honest enough to admit our mistakes.

People also use the phrase "being consistent," however, when they mean "sticking to what you say." This is an important part of consistency. We call it "following through," and explain it in the next chapter.

Kids like to know where they stand

Setting limits

- Limits tell kids what they may and may not do.
- Limits must be fair and reasonable.
- Set limits in advance when possible.
- Set limits that fit the child — different kids need different limits.
- Emphasize what kids *can* do.
- Give positive options: "You can't play the drum, but if you feel like pounding you can use your wooden peg set — it's quieter."
- Be reasonably consistent.
- Set limits *you* can live with.
- Prevent the need for limits whenever you can.
  - Baby/child-proof your home.
  - Provide safe play areas.
  - Teach good behavior.

Guideline

Let your kids know where they stand by setting reasonable, age-appropriate limits around their behavior.

Chapter Three

Setting consequences and following through

Remember Popeye? One of the lines he used to sing was, "I says what I means, I means what I says, I'm Popeye the sailor man." As kids we loved that line — and we loved Popeye. He was somebody solid, somebody we could trust.

Most of us assume we do, indeed, mean what we say and say what we mean, and we would be shocked if we thought we were lying to our children or misleading them in any way. Unfortunately many of us do just that countless times a day without realizing it. Here's an example: Jeremy is bouncing his ball near his baby brother's head. His mother asks him to stop. He keeps right on bouncing the ball, so she explains that she'll have to take the ball away if he doesn't stop. Jeremy continues the bouncing. And what does his mother do? Nothing. Or maybe she screams at him. But she doesn't take the ball away. When Jeremy's mother deals with his misbehavior in this way time and again, it sends a very clear message to him: "My mom doesn't mean what she says." He concludes, quite logically, that it doesn't really matter whether he stays within the limits his mother sets.

Following through with what we say we are going to do is critically important in dealing with children. Often, the problem is not that we neglect to tell kids what's going to happen if they don't do what we ask; many adults spend a lot of time shouting things like, "If you bounce that ball one more time, I'm going to take it away." The problem is that when the ball is bounced again nobody takes it away. When we explain to a child what the consequence of his misbehavior is going be — and we are certain it is a just, reasonable, and appropriate consequence — it is absolutely essential that we carry it out.

What we mean by "consequences"

Different people mean different things when they talk about the use of consequences as a child-rearing technique, so Dr. Kason and I want to explain carefully what we mean by the term. First, let's look at three terms: punishment, discipline, and consequences. Generally, punishment is defined as an action that a child finds unpleasant and that is aimed at changing his behavior. When we use this definition, punishment doesn't sound like such a bad thing

— and it doesn't have to be. But for many people, the word carries a great deal of emotional baggage. They tend to think of punishment as something that is hurtful or even harmful. The term to discipline, which expresses the same general idea as to punish, doesn't seem to suffer from so many negative connotations. In everyday language, a consequence is the result of an action. In the fields of parenting and teaching, the word's meaning has broadened. Now we talk about setting a consequence, which means we tell a child what the result of misbehaving will be. This consequence might be the natural result of his misbehavior, or it might be a form of discipline we have chosen.

Dr. Kason and I think it is much easier to think in positive terms about setting a consequence than about punishing. For us, a consequence is well thought out; it is explained in advance whenever possible; it is logical and appropriate. It never hurts a child, physically or emotionally. It does help him learn that his actions bring results, and that there will be times as he goes through life when he will need to consider his actions carefully.

We break the concept of consequences into three categories: natural consequences, logical consequences, and appropriate consequences. Different schools of thought in parenting sometimes have different ways of defining these terms. For Dr. Kason and I, natural consequence is one that would be the natural result of a certain action if no one did anything to interrupt the flow of events. If, for instance, a child refuses to pick up his dirty clothes and put them in the clothes hamper, and if his parents don't give in and do it for him, the natural consequence will be that, eventually, he will not have any clean clothes to wear.

Several parenting schools use this — or a slightly different — definition for a natural consequence. There is no doubt a natural consequence can be very effective. But some parents aren't comfortable with letting the often lengthy scenarios that develop play all the way out. And not all situations are safe or appropriate for the use of natural consequences. Dr. Kason recently met a young mother who had heard the term natural consequences discussed, but had not bothered to find out what it meant in terms of parenting; she had defined it in a literal sense. Thus, rather than structuring her child's environment or establishing guidelines for behavior, she simply let him reap the natural consequences of his actions. She reasoned he would learn, for instance, not to touch the stove — not because she told him not to, but because he would burn his hand when he did. Rather than tucking away the cords of lamps, she left them hanging, reasoning that once he pulled on one and saw the lamp come toppling toward him, he would never do it again. The child did, of course, eventually pull on the cord and was injured when the lamp crashed down on his head. This is clearly not an appropriate way to use the concept of natural consequences. No consequence should ever threaten a child's well-being.

Logical consequences relate in a logical and reasonable way to a child's misbehavior. For example, if your seventeen-year-old son gets a speeding ticket, he will have to pay the ticket himself, and he might lose his privilege to drive the car for a number of days or weeks. The logical consequence of a five-year-old boy's coloring on the wall would be that he has to clean, or at least help clean, the wall. Taking a toy away from a child for a specific time when she misuses it is also a logical consequence. If a little girl takes the caboose of her toy train off its track and runs it across the teak coffee table, her father might tell her she must either play with the caboose properly or have it taken away for the rest of the day.

Appropriate consequences are very similar, but they may not be quite so directly related to the misbehavior. Here are a few scenarios in which appropriate consequences are used. A five-year-old is tugging on his three-year-old sister's new toy. His mother tells him to stop pulling at the toy or he will have to go sit in a chair and take a "time out" for three minutes. A father finds his five-year-old daughter in the yard eating a cookie. He asks where she got it, and discovers she took it off the neighbors' picnic table without asking. He tells her she must immediately tell the neighbor what she has done and apologize.

Before we explain how to set consequences, we need to discuss when — and if — they are needed. We don't want to give the impression you need to issue warnings about every transgression your child might eventually think up: "If you ever try to slide a bologna sandwich into the VCR, you won't be allowed to watch TV for a week!" "If you put Krazy

Setting consequences and following through

Glue on the TV buttons, you won't ever get to watch TV again!" These warnings would create a negative environment — and they might give your kids a lot of intriguing ideas!

When to set consequences

One logical time to set a consequence is when you set a limit. For instance, you can say, "Please don't bounce that ball by the baby's head. If you do, I'll have to take the ball away for the rest of the afternoon." But setting a consequence before the child starts to do anything wrong is not always a good idea, because it can give the child the impression you thoroughly *expect* him to break the limit you're setting.

There are, of course, occasions when it makes sense to set limits and consequences at the same time. One is when you are explaining the rules for an outing for a group of kids; this helps you structure the activity more firmly than you would need to do with only one or two children. Another is when you know a child will be tempted to do something. You might say, "Evan, I can see you really want that plane Joey just got for his birthday, but you're going to have to wait. You have the choice of waiting nicely — maybe you could play with your Transformers while you do — or going to sit in that chair over there for a while. I hope you can wait." It is also appropriate to set a limit and a consequence at the same time when you are dealing with a limit that has been broken before.

As a rule of thumb, however, it's much better to explain the behavior you expect without mentioning any consequence. That way you make it clear you assume the child is going to cooperate. Then, when and if your observations tell you he just might be contemplating breaking the limit, you calmly restate the limit, perhaps this time explaining the consequence. For instance, when you notice that Evan has just scooted a few feet closer to Joey, has his arm stretched out, his eye on the plane and a covetous look on his face, it is a perfect time to remind Evan he's going to have to wait and to tell him what will happen if he doesn't. We call this kind of observation troubleshooting, and give you more pointers in Chapter Ten.

Occasionally, there will be times when you will need to carry out a consequence that has not been set in advance. All children, at one time or another, do unacceptable things that were not forbidden in advance. When this happens you can give some thought to the matter and lay down a consequence that seems reasonable. Or you might want to use the opportunity to sit down with the child for awhile and, together, determine what an appropriate consequence might be.

Children like reminders and choices

Children will often give you a clue that it's time to remind them about a limit and to explain the consequences of breaking it. They often want you to do this because it helps them stop themselves before the limit is broken. If, for instance, a group of children need to keep relatively quiet, you can set the limit once, then remind them about it as soon you hear the noise level go up a bit: "Hey, kids, it is starting to get a little noisy. Remember you have to keep quiet because the baby's sleeping. That's much better. Thanks!" Then, "Whoops, it's starting to get noisy again. Please keep at that nice, quiet level you were talking at a minute ago or you're all going to have to go outside."

The way you word the consequence is also important. In my work with children over the years, I have found that it is more effective to offer a choice than to set down an ultimatum. In other words, saying something like, "You can either stay here and play gently with your brother — no hitting — or go sit in the chair for five minutes. Which will it be?" is usually preferable to, "If you try to hit your brother again, you'll have to sit it the chair." Sometimes, it is also effective to present a third positive alternative, "You can either take the drum outside or play quietly here in the living room. If you pound the drum in here I'll have to put it away for the rest of the day. Maybe you'd like to play with your Lego set in here. That's quiet."

You'll notice that it takes more time to convey the consequences you set in this way than it does to shout a command. Sometimes having the time to rationally discuss the consequences of your child's misbehavior with him is a luxury you can't afford, and there will be times when a bald statement like, "Stop poking your brother or go sit in the chair," will probably have to do. Offering choices and alternatives whenever possible is, however, more effective. We'll tell you more about offering choices in Chapter Six.

Some people feel you should never state a consequence by saying, "If you do that, I'll do this." They believe this is a threat. While Dr. Kason and I agree it's not always the best way to word a consequence, we don't think of it as a threat — not if what you're planning to do is just and reasonable, and if you carry it out.

Why it's hard to follow through

Once you have set a limit and the consequence of breaking that limit has been clearly defined, you must follow through with the consequence as soon as the limit is broken. For example, as soon as the group of children who were told to keep quiet were making too much noise you would say, ""Sorry, kids, but that's it. Everybody outside. No, you can't have one more chance, I reminded you twice about the noise." Period. That's it. Out they go.

It sounds simple. But why, oh, why, is it so difficult to *do* what you say you're going to do? There are at least three reasons. First, some of us are afraid the children won't like us if we inflict anything unpleasant on them. Second, some of us are afraid the children will think we don't like them if we make them do anything they don't want to do. Third, we sometimes wonder whether the consequence we have set is really fair.

We all want children to love us. To be loved by children is a special badge of honor. For those of you who are afraid children won't like you if you have to discipline them in any way, Dr. Kason and I can offer you reassurance. Neither of us, in all our years of experience, has had a child stop liking us just because we carried out an appropriate consequence. We have found, instead, that children gained respect for us and felt increasingly secure in their relationships with us when they found that we said what we meant and we meant what we said. Even though children often kick up a fuss when they have to suffer the unpleasant consequences of their misbehavior, there is never any lasting problem if the adult has been playing fair, setting limits and consequences that are clear, just and reasonable.

Many parents hesitate to follow through with consequences because they are afraid their children will think they aren't loved. Some teachers are slack on discipline because they are afraid their pupils will think they don't care about them. Usually, this fear is unfounded — as long as the consequences are just and the adults have done their best to create a warm, loving environment.

It is, however, possible for children to get the idea that we don't love them when we punish them. One of the most important factors in preventing this is to make sure, when we are dealing with behavior problems, that we always make it clear to the child that it is the *misbehavior* we dislike, not the child.

I love you, but not what you're doing

Parents and teachers of young children often make the mistake of saying, "You're a bad boy!" to a child who has *done* something wrong. If you tell a child he is "bad" or "naughty" or "rotten" or "a pain in the neck" every time he makes a mistake or displeases you, he can get the idea that you don't love or like him.

Children are often much more perceptive than we think. Most of them figure out, by an early age, that very few people in the real world have much esteem for anyone who is thought to be bad. Once a child has made this observation, he can easily draw the conclusion that the people who continually tell him he is bad must not like him very much. The problem can be more serious than this. If a child hears it often enough, he may become convinced that he really is bad and his self-esteem may plummet. This can have a negative effect that results in the child's behavior becoming more and more unmanageable as his self-esteem circles downward.

There are ways to express your displeasure with a child's actions without damaging his self-image. These methods are positive and effective. Since children don't like to hear about how bad they are, they tend to shut out any message worded in this way and miss the point the adult is trying to make about their behavior. A child is far more likely to listen when he knows it is misbehavior that is being criticized, not his self, and that he will continue to be loved and accepted in spite of his actions.

The issue of acceptance is central. The renowned psychologist Carl Rogers made people aware of the importance of something he called *unconditional love*. When you withhold your love from a child because his behavior displeases you, you are putting conditions on your love. You are saying, in effect, "I will only love you if you behave the way I want you to." Dr. Kason and I believe children thrive best when they grow up knowing that the important people in their lives love them without any strings attached. This doesn't mean that you don't ever get angry, that you don't ever lose your patience, or that you don't ever mean it when you shout you've had all you can take. But it does mean that your love, at the bottom of your heart, is an absolutely constant thing, and that, more importantly, your children know it.

Let's look at how you might handle your two-year-old daughter if she has just hit her little brother. Instead of telling her she's a bad girl, you might say, "No. Don't hit." Then take her hand firmly and add, "If you try to hit again, you will have to go sit in a chair for two minutes." If the child is older, you could say, "Hitting is not a good thing to do. You can play without hitting here with us or you can go play in the living room by yourself." If the child is old enough to know that hitting is never allowed, you can carry out a standard consequence immediately without a warning: "Hitting isn't allowed. You know that. You'll have to go to your room until you can show me you are ready to play nicely. You can come down in ten minutes and try again." Another choice, if the child is old enough to understand, is to express your feelings. "I get very angry when I see you hit your brother because it hurts him. Hitting is not acceptable. You'll have to go sit in the kitchen for ten minutes."

Phrases such as, "That's not allowed," "That's not acceptable," "I get upset when you do that," or,

"No, you must not do that!" are just a few of the hundreds of the workable alternatives to saying, "You're a bad girl," or, "You're a naughty boy." These alternatives explain what you really mean to say much more clearly and are, therefore, more effective. Another advantage of expressing yourself in this manner is that you won't need to worry about whether your child will think you don't love him when you have to discipline him. He'll know that your love is constant and accepting no matter what he does. This will make it easier for you to follow through when you set consequences.

Are you sure the consequence is fair?

The third reason we find it difficult to follow through is that we sometimes worry about whether a consequence is just and reasonable. Of course, no one should ever, under any circumstances, carry out an unreasonable consequence. The difficulty arises when the consequence is reasonable but the parent or teacher isn't sure about it. The reason this happens so often is probably that no collective experience in our own childhood leaves a more lasting impression, or a more damaging scar, than the way we were punished. Very few things anger a child more than feeling he has been unjustly treated.

It is clearly necessary that we take a deep look at our feelings about punishment and how we were punished as a child. We need to keep in mind the fact that we will tend, in times of stress, to automatically use the words and actions that were used against us when we were children.

Setting consequences and following through

In addition, we must carefully consider each consequence we set. A just and reasonable consequence does not hurt a child emotionally or physically; it never frightens him; it never threatens him, and it never makes him think less of himself — or less of you.

Since it is sometimes difficult to think of a fair consequence when you are angry or extremely upset at a child's misbehavior, it can be helpful if you keep a stockpile of consequences in your mind. We provide a list of consequences in the next chapter that we have found helpful.

Always keep in mind the fact that if the action you take is not fair, a child will not learn anything from it. Because children have a keen sense of justice they get caught up in the indignation they feel at being unjustly treated and completely miss the point you are trying to make. The mother of an emotionally disturbed boy I worked with told me that as a child she had sometimes been locked out of her home for hours on end as a punishment. She could recall many details about these occurrences: how the paint was peeling from the door as she stood pounding at it, how the pounding hurt her hand, what the weather was like, and how overwhelming the rage she felt was. She could recall everything — except what it was she was being punished for. To this day she has no idea what specific behavior her parents were trying to change.

In an ideal world we could do away with the whole question of consequences and everything that smacks of punishment. Indeed, it is our contention that by letting children know where they stand and what is expected of them, by providing lots of appropriate outlets for their rambunctiousness, and by giving enough affection and positive feedback, a great deal of unacceptable behavior can be avoided. Still, there will be times when the law has to be laid down and carried out. When that time comes there are a few factors that need to be considered.

Different kids need different consequences

Once we have given adequate thought to the appropriateness of a certain consequence, we need to think about the individual differences we find in children. There are kids who will almost never need to have consequences mentioned to them. For these children, explaining what you expect from them and reminding them of what you asked, in the event that they do start to slip up, is usually enough. One of the children who plays a very important part in my life is a good example of this. The closest she ever came to being punished in her first six years of life was for someone to remind her that she was coming close to breaking a limit or to say, in a rather stern voice, "Heather, I asked you to stop that!" Many other children will stop an undesirable behavior when you take the time to reason with them. You simply need to explain why they shouldn't be doing something and they stop. Presto! Still other children only need to be reminded of what's expected of them from time to time; they sincerely want to keep within the limits you've set, but in their exuberance, they forget.

These mild techniques work on some children most of the time, and they work on all children some of the time. It is generally a good idea to give the child the benefit of the doubt and provide him with an opportunity to respond to a mild approach before using a stronger one.

Dr. Kason and I call this the incremental approach. You give the child more and more information, a bit at a time, as needed. Here's an example of how it works. Suppose you take your kids on a picnic, only to discover that the water is high and running dangerously fast in the creek they are usually allowed to play near. First, you explain the behavior you expect. You might say, "I'm sorry, kids, but you can't play near the water today. In fact, I want you stay fairly far away from it. Just so you're clear what I mean, let's say it's okay for you to play where there's grass, but the sandy part that runs along the edge of the water is too close. Understand? You are not to play on the sandy part today." Next, you share your reasoning. "Do you notice how much faster the water is flowing than usual? That makes it quite dangerous. Even a very strong swimmer couldn't handle that water! That's why I want you to stay farther away than usual." You then keep one eye on the children as they begin to play. When one ventures a little too close to the sandy bank for you to be comfortable, you use it as an opportunity to remind them all about the limit. "Hey, Stacey! You're starting to get pretty close to that sandy area. That really makes me nervous. Remember what I said about not getting near the sandy bank!" When she moves away, thank her for being cooperative and for setting a good example for the other kids.

Involve kids in decision making

An effective variation on this approach is to get the kids involved at the reasoning stage and let them help you decide on the limit. You can start a discussion about how the water looks different. One kid might say it looks scary, and from this point you can lead them into making a decision about what might be a safe boundary. Then when Stacey gets close to the water you can say, "Stacey, remember we decided it wouldn't be safe to play on the sand today." When and if it starts to become apparent that the children are not going to heed your warning, you immediately restate the limit and add the consequence: "No playing past where the grass stops. If one of you steps on the sand, you'll have to come up here, sit on the blanket and take a five-minute time out from playing."

In general, it is a good idea to involve the children in the thinking out and the setting of limits whenever you can. That way you don't have to be the heavy, and they get valuable experience. Interestingly enough, I often found in my years of teaching that the children tended to set much tougher limits and consequences for themselves than I would have.

In the next chapter, we go over the stockpile of consequences we have come to be comfortable with and examine a few we don't think are appropriate in any circumstances.

Setting consequences and following through

Setting consequences

- Consequences are what happens to a child when she misbehaves.
- Make sure the consequences you set are just and reasonable.
- Always follow through with the consequences you set.
- Make sure the child knows you love him even when you don't like what he's doing.
- Hints on setting consequences:

  ▪ Set the consequence either when you set the limit or when you sense a limit is about to be broken.

  ▪ Remember that different consequences work better with different kids.

  ▪ Give kids reminders whenever you think they're about to break a limit.

  ▪ Get kids involved in setting limits and consequences whenever possible.

  ▪ Give kids a choice: "Do you want to stay here and play quietly or do you want to take a time out for five minutes?"

  ▪ Remember to consider your wording when you offer a choice. There is a big difference between saying, "Quit messing with your food or go to your room!" and, "Do you want to stay here and eat politely or leave the table for a time out?"

When you have trouble following through

- ❏ You might simply be afraid your kids won't like you. If so, remember that when you follow through with consequences that are fair and reasonable, your kids will learn to trust you and what you say.

- ❏ You might be afraid your kids will think you don't love them. If so, remember that this won't happen — as long as you have created an atmosphere of unconditional love in your home.

Guideline

Say what you mean, mean what you say. Explain consequences clearly. If a child breaks a limit, follow through!

Chapter Four

Facing the consequences

When Dr. Kason was a new mother she had a disturbing experience. One day while she and a few other young mothers were discussing the question of discipline, she casually mentioned the fact that she planned to raise her son without spanking him. She got some very strong reactions from the other women. One mother said, "But you'll spoil him!" Another said, "But if you don't spank him, how will you let him know he's done something wrong?" A third asked, "How will you keep him from running in the road and things?" Clearly, these mothers equated discipline with spanking. Dr. Kason was surprised that apparently it had never occurred to these parents that there could be *alternatives* to spanking, or that different approaches might be more effective.

These alternatives are what we call consequences. One of the difficulties in using them effectively is being able to think of an appropriate one quickly when you are in the middle of a tense situation with a child. When I was working with troubled children and constantly dealing with behavior problems, I often found I didn't have time to give much thought to what a consequence was going to be before I set it. Parents often have this problem, especially if there is more than one child around. In order to solve this difficulty for myself, I developed a little stockpile of consequences over the years. This helped me have a reasonable, fair response on the tip of my tongue when I was in the midst of handling a behavior problem. Dr. Kason and I have come up with a number of consequences that, in our experience, have worked particularly well. We also mention some forms of punishment we feel are inappropriate.

Taking away the toy

Taking a toy away from a child can be a very effective consequence. It is especially appropriate when the toy has somehow been involved in the controversy, for example, the ball that is bounced too close to the baby's head, the drum that is played ad nauseum or the new truck two children are fighting over. The trouble with this consequence is that, surprisingly enough, it is very tough to carry out. There are a couple of reasons for this. One is that taking a toy away from a child makes you feel like a big meanie. The other is that once the toy has been gone for about two seconds, children invariably begin to act like angels, which makes you think you should relent and give the toy back. Of course, as long as you know the consequence you set was reasonable, you should not give in. One of the ways to avoid this situation is to cushion the way you state the consequence with a time limit. You might say, "I'm going to have to take the ball away for half an hour," or, "I'm taking the ball away until you show me you can play nicely together with the other toys here." The latter alternative gives you a chance to give the toy back after you are sure they have settled down.

If you have explained you are going to take the toy away for a specific amount of time, stick to your time limit. When the children begin to play nicely and ask if they can have the ball back before the time is up, they are testing you. To handle the situation positively, put the focus back on them. Compliment them on how well they are playing together, remind them that they have to wait only so many more minutes until they get the ball back, suggest alternative things for them to do in the meantime — but don't give in! Be sure, instead, that the consequence is just and reasonable before you set it.

Taking a time out

Having a child stop the activity she is involved in and take what has come to be called "time out" for a few minutes can be a very effective strategy in a wide variety of situations. In fact, some experts in parenting and teaching feel a time out is the only consequence you ever need to use. It falls into the category of what Dr. Kason and I call appropriate consequences. It is particularly useful when two children are beginning to squabble. When you notice tension starting to build up between the children you might say, "Girls, I get the feeling there's a fight brewing here. Please settle down and speak nicely to each other." If the tension continues to mount, you can say, "I don't want you two to get into a fight. Please stop arguing right now, or you'll both have to take a time out." If they don't stop, say, "That's it. Time out for three minutes. Laurie, you go sit on the couch. Jessie, you sit in the chair. I'll tell you when the time is up."

One of the reasons a time out works is that, during it, the child is not getting any attention from you or the other children. Nor does she get any other positive feedback: it is a quiet time. She is not allowed to talk, play or make noise during the time out. A time out also removes the child from the source of tension and gives her a chance to cool down. For most children it seems like a fair consequence, and they can accept it without much fuss — they know even their favorite hockey players have to sit in the penalty box once in a while. Some parents and teachers even set aside an area that is known as the penalty box. It might only be a chair in a corner (it never is an actual, closed-in box a child must get into), but the name gives it an aura that a child — particularly one interested in sports — takes seriously.

Go sit in that chair

This consequence is a slightly more structured version of the time out. It is so mild you might think it wouldn't do any good at all. For many children, however, it works very well. And it brings up an interesting point: a consequence does not have to be at all harsh or severe to work. Often, the fact that the child has to do something she doesn't want to do is all it takes to turn an everyday occurrence into a consequence.

In my many years of working with troubled and average children, I used this consequence more than any other with children under the age of twelve and found it to be particularly effective. The chair can be anywhere, but it is usually best if it is located away from the center of activity. Depending on the child and the disruptiveness of her behavior, the chair might be only a few feet away, for example, at the opposite end of the table from where an activity is going on. Or it might need to be located in another room. If the other children are moving around freely, the chair could be in the midst of things, and still do the trick. It is essential that the child remain quiet and refrain from interacting with the other children or the adult until the time is up.

The adult in charge should usually set a specific time for the "sitting." Keep in mind that it is difficult for young children to sit still for even a short time. For young children, a wind-up kitchen timer set for a specified number of minutes can be helpful. This prevents arguing about whether the time is up, and waiting for the bell to go off gives the child something concrete to focus on. Dr. Marianne Neifert, author of the excellent book *Dr. Mom*, recommends one minute per year of age. Thus maximum time out for a five-year-old is five minutes. If the time limit is beyond the child's endurance, she will jump up, and there will be another misbehavior to deal with.

Come back when you're ready

An alternative to setting a specific time is to tell the child to sit in the segregated chair until she thinks she is able to work quietly or play nicely. This provides the child with an opportunity to take responsibility for her own behavior. It also keeps the parent or teacher from being the only one who imposes the punishment.

Scotty was a ten-year-old boy I worked with who had been expelled from the regular school system and from special classes for problem children because his teachers could not handle him. But once he was given an opportunity to decide when he had had enough time out, he began to respond positively to discipline. His story also provides a good example of how we can help children learn to take a time out if they resist the idea in the beginning.

When Scotty disrupted children who were doing their lessons at our clinic, I would say, "Scotty, please sit in the chair on the other side of the door until you feel you are able to work quietly with us here." If Scotty didn't hop up immediately and go, I would take him gently to the chair. The first few times I had to sit beside him, encouraging him to stay by keeping my hand on his arm and asking, "Do you think you are ready to come back and work quietly with us now?" When he agreed, I would say, "Good, go back and show me now."

Once Scotty learned that I meant it when I told him to go to the chair, he would go on his own — it was less embarrassing than having his teacher sitting there practically holding his hand! As his behavior improved, the amount of time he had to stay in the chair decreased. Eventually, whenever I thought Scotty might be on the verge of disrupting the class, I could help him get control of himself by saying, "Scotty, do you want to stay here and work quietly or would you rather sit in the other room for a minute?"

I believe Scotty was able to respond to this form of discipline because he could take an active role in it; this freed him from his overpowering desire to rebel against authority. Also, the respite he got by separating himself from the other children gave him the time he needed to cool off. The chance to set his own time limit allowed him to save face without having to act like he was tough.

Go sit in the corner

There are a number of variations on the go-sit-in-the-chair theme. Our grandparents and their parents before them used the sit-in-the-corner technique. It's still a good option, because it separates the child effectively from the interesting things in the room but still keeps her within your sight. But I don't use this technique. I have too many painful memories of sitting for what seemed like endless hours in the corner of a classroom hearing real or imagined snickers behind my back. But the technique in itself is not harmful, and Dr. Kason is very comfortable with it when it is used properly. This brings us to an essential point about having a child sit in a chair, a corner, or another room: the idea is not to ostracize the child in any way; it is simply to temporarily separate her — in a psychological and physical manner — from the activity and the people she has been disrupting.

One of the beauties of separating a child in this manner is that it often gives a child time she may need to think. Recently I was caring for two boys, a six-year-old and a five-year-old, whose parents are separated and beginning the process of divorce. The two of them and another five-year-old were playing with play dough at the kitchen table. Quite suddenly the six-year-old began to disrupt the two five-year-olds. I asked him to stop. As his disruptions started to intensify, I explained that he could either stop interrupting the others or go sit in a chair in the living room for five minutes. Instead, he took two chairs from the table, placed them in the corner and stretched out on them with his back to the room.

Belatedly, I realized the underlying cause of his misbehavior. The children had been constructing play dough people, making up stories about them, and acting them out. Some of the stories had begun to sound very much like the problems that were going on at home. Since this is a normal, and generally healthy, way children work through and relieve some of the frustrations they encounter in life, I hadn't interrupted or made any comments. However, in this case, the playacting had suddenly touched on areas the older boy was not ready to deal with. Because he couldn't quite put his feelings into words, he resorted to disruptive behavior. He was telling me he needed a time out from what was going on at the table. Still, he wanted to hear the things his younger brother was saying, and he clearly didn't want to be alone. It would have been detrimental for me to insist that he go to the other room simply because that was what I had originally said. He was taking the required time out, but he was structuring it in a way that suited his needs. Once I realized what was going on, I spoke to him quietly and reassuringly, but I didn't intrude on his space. When he decided to come back to the table he crawled onto my lap; I held and comforted him for a long time, for that was what he was telling me he needed then.

This is a perfect example of how disruptive behavior is often a child's way of expressing her need for something she cannot put into words. When these situations arise, it is important that we tune into what our children are really trying to tell us and respond accordingly. Usually it is best to carry out any consequence that has been set, since this reaffirms the child's sense of security. Still, we need to know when to be flexible and adaptable so we can provide whatever else — in addition to security — is being asked for.

Other alternatives

Another variation on the go-sit-in-the-chair technique is sending a child to her room. This works well if the room isn't a haven of toys and electronic delights. In our opinion, however, it is a consequence that should not be overused, especially with very young children. It can make the room seem like an unhappy place. This can make bedtime seem like a punishment. It can also make a young child feel like she is being pushed away or deserted. We do not believe children should be locked in their bedrooms. If a child refuses to stay in her room, a parent can stay in the room and hold the child or stand outside the door and hold it shut for the specified time limit. Generally, once a child learns she really does have to stay in her room until the time is up, she will stay on her own.

A young mother I know, who is caring for her four-year-old daughter and providing day care for three others, came up with a creative alternative to having a misbehaving child sit in a corner. She calls it the "seventh step." When any of the children become too disruptive, they have to leave the playroom and walk up the stairs to the seventh step. They sit there for a specified amount of time, or until they feel they are ready to come back and play nicely. The mother says the seventh step is an excellent consequence for her to use because it separates the child completely from the enjoyable activities, but it also makes it possible for the mother to keep an eye on the young offender through the posts on the staircase. She adds that the children consider going to the seventh step a serious event, and that she sometimes has to hide her face so they don't see her smile when she hears a sad, solemn little voice counting from one to seven on the way up.

Losing privileges

Taking away privileges can be either a logical or appropriate consequence. It is workable as long as the child is old enough to associate her misbehavior with a punishment that might come later. In other words, telling a four-year-old she can't watch cartoons at five o'clock when she marks on the wall at ten in the morning isn't going to work. By the time five o'clock rolls around she will have forgotten what she did wrong, she'll throw a fuss about not being able to watch the cartoons, and you'll have another discipline problem on your hands. More importantly, however, she will not be able to associate the misbehavior with the consequence — too much time will have elapsed. (The same is true of telling a child her father will punish her when he gets home. This is, in addition, a very unfair thing to do to the father!)

For older children taking away privileges can be both effective and appropriate. If a teenager gets a speeding ticket, taking away her car privileges for a specified time helps underline the seriousness of what she has done.

In one educational clinic I worked in, we structured each forty-five-minute learning period so that there were ten minutes of free time at the end. Each child earned her free time by accomplishing a reasonable, preset amount of schoolwork or maintaining an agreed-upon level of behavior for the first thirty-five minutes. If the goals were not met or if behavior broke down, the child lost her chance at having the privilege of that particular free time.

This consequence only works if the privilege is something the child really cares about. If you are setting clear, reasonable limits in advance and the loss of a privilege — whether it is watching TV, use of the car or the loss of freedom in general, as in grounding — doesn't have any effect on your child's behavior, it is probably because it is something she can get along fairly happily without or has come up with a substitute for. For example, if you tell your teenager she can't watch television one evening and she is just as happy listening to music in her room, the consequence won't have much effect. But don't give up on the whole idea — try fishing around until you discover what works.

Repairing the damage

Having a child repair any damage her misbehavior may have caused is also an excellent logical consequence. It often goes hand in hand with losing a privilege. My five-year-old goddaughter recently marked on the walls with a set of washable markers. She had to help her mother clean the walls, and she also lost the privilege of keeping the markers in her room until she could convince her parents that she could use them properly.

If the child is old enough to clean up, repair, or pay for the damage by herself, then she should. Many of us probably remember having to save our allowance until we could pay for a window we broke while carelessly throwing a ball. When we were a little older, we might have lost our driving privileges and had to take a few extra jobs until we could pay for a fender we dented on the car. Such consequences, when they are properly used, improve children's behavior and help them develop a sense of responsibility.

Don't scold — discuss!

Scolding is the most used and most singularly ineffective method of handling a misbehaving child. Nobody likes getting scolded. It hurts our ears, so we just turn our ears off! Who among us hasn't learned, by a very early age, to block out what we don't want to hear? An adult-child discussion is a different matter. In it you take the time to sit down with the child and help her understand what was unacceptable about her behavior. You help her figure out for herself how the problem could have been prevented and how she can improve her behavior in the future. In order to be effective, this type of discussion should always result in the child clearly understanding both what her limits are and what the consequences will be if she repeats the misbehavior.

Adult-child discussions can, with fairly compliant children and with those who are highly motivated to please, often replace the need for any other type of consequence. And they work with almost all children at least some of the time.

Scolding, however, almost never works. Especially when a child knows that, if she misbehaves again, all she is going to get is another scolding. Can you imagine yelling at a child and saying, "If you do that once more I'm going to yell at you again!" This, however, is the hidden message behind most scoldings.

Never ever threaten

Scoldings often include threats; an adult-child discussion never does. Indeed, a child should never, under any circumstance, be threatened. To threaten a child, in our definition, is to tell her something terrible will happen to her if she doesn't do what you want: "I'll kill you if you touch that toy again," "I'm going to walk away and leave you for good if you don't stop that crying," "I'll beat you within an inch of your life if you try that again." While you may have no intention of carrying out your threats, the child does not know that.

A threat terrifies the child and causes her to lose her faith in you and in any reasonable consequence you might set in the future. Threats are clearly so detrimental that it is hard to believe any caring adult would ever use them against a child. But you only have to walk down the aisles of a store crowded with parents and children to hear any number of them.

Such statements can do untold harm to innocent, trusting children. A very close friend of mine has told us a story about a threat that was used repeatedly in her family. Many years ago, when her two brothers were rambunctious, school-age boys, her parents developed a dreadful form of punishment. When they thought the boys had been particularly bad, they would put them in the car and drive them to the local orphanage. They would then tell them that, if they didn't improve their behavior immediately, they would be left on the front steps. Both boys grew up to be suicidal alcoholics. While we are not saying this cruel treatment was the cause of their alcoholism, the threats certainly could have been a factor in creating the deep-seated insecurity so often found in an alcoholic's past.

To spank or not to spank

This is undoubtedly the most controversial issue in child rearing today. While many — but unfortunately not all — schools have done away with the strap and the paddle, spanking is still the only form of punishment in many homes. We hope we have offered you enough alternatives to the use of bodily punishment that you will never need to use it.

Most contemporary child psychologists agree that spanking is, at best, an ineffective form of punishment. The child is often so angry at being mistreated that she misses the entire point the parent is trying to make. Spanking that hurts a child can cause her to lose her trust in her parents. The line between spanking a child and child abuse is very thin, and it is far too easy, in the heat of rage, to cross it. It is better, we think, to avoid spanking altogether. Those few psychologists who are not totally against spanking generally recommend using it extremely sparingly and only as a last resort. If you believe spanking is necessary, you might want to consider doing it only when the limit that has been broken is one that endangers the child's life — for example, when the child has been swimming in a dangerous river near your home that she knows she is not allowed to go near. And there are a few guidelines that can help you make sure you are not abusing your child. Spank only a fully clothed child, and only on the buttocks. Or try lightly rapping a child on the hand as an alternative — other than this, never strike a child's bare skin. Try never to spank when you are close to being in a rage — it's too easy to lose control. Never use any kind of object — a strap, a stick, a brush; use only your bare hand. You are abusing your child if you leave any kind of mark on her. In fact, spanking should not hurt the child at all. A smack on a well-padded bottom or a tap on the knuckles can get your point across — if you can't think of another way — without the child feeling any pain at all. She will be upset enough by the fact that you have struck her. Still, we urge you to use the alternatives. A home without spanking does not have to be a home without discipline.

Inappropriate consequences

Unfortunately, even the most reasonable consequence can be twisted into a cruel punishment. There is a huge difference between sending a child to her room and locking her in it; between telling a child she has to take her drum outside and locking the door after her; between making her sit in a chair for five minutes and making her sit for an hour. I had a teacher once who turned standing in the corner into a form of torture. Whenever this teacher caught children chewing gum in her grade-six class, she would draw a circle on the blackboard, take the gum and stick it in the center of the circle. She would then make the gum chewer stand with her nose stuck on the gum. Not only did this humiliate the child, it also caused great pain, for the teacher would draw the circle at a height the child could reach only by stretching her legs or standing on tiptoe. After ten or fifteen minutes of standing like this, the pain was excruciating.

For most of us the difference between a cruel punishment and a reasonable consequence is obvious — as long as we are sitting quietly thinking about the matter. When we are under excessive stress, however, even the most caring, reasonable adult is capable of doing something he regrets later. Both parents and teachers must guard against this.

This is especially true for anyone who was cruelly treated as a child. It is very difficult, when we are under stress, to keep ourselves from falling back on the words and actions that were used on us when we were children. If you are in doubt about a consequence, don't use it. You can check the lists of appropriate and inappropriate consequences at the end of this chapter.

Children create stress

We shouldn't kid ourselves: children do create stress. Great amounts of it. Parents and teachers have been saying this for generations, but many of us don't discover it for ourselves until we've already started our families. For this reason, we think it's appropriate to digress for a moment and talk about how stressful child rearing can be. This is especially important because so much of the current talk about child rearing centers on how *wonderful* it is to have children, how *fascinating* they are, and how *fulfilling* it is to have them. Children are all these marvelous things and more. They are also difficult, they are demanding, and their presence completely changes our lives. As a new father we know put it: "Why didn't anybody tell me it was going to be like this?"

He added that everyone, their family physician included, had told his wife and him that they must take a prenatal course, but no one had suggested they take a parenting course. "But," he said, "everything we spent all those weeks in the prenatal classes preparing for was over in twelve hours — and now that the baby's a few months old I've suddenly discovered all the changes have thrown *me* into a personal crisis and *us* into a marital crisis. I was totally unprepared for it."

The changes begin with pregnancy — and they are not just bodily and hormonal changes. Both parents often experience a kind of identity crisis. Dr. Kason says that when she was pregnant her friends and colleagues began to treat her differently. Friends would call less and apologize when they did. Colleagues were suddenly concerned about whether she was too tired or overdoing it. Much of the concern was reassuring, and the attention was pleasant. Still, people treated her as if she were a different person.

And she was. In addition to the doctor, professor, wife, and friend roles she had become accustomed to over the years, she was about to take on the role of mother. The same sorts of things can occur to men when their wives become pregnant. Tradition tells them they must grow up, settle down, and become the breadwinner once they become a father. The new father we mentioned said, "I went crazy at work, working overtime, trying to take on all kinds of new responsibilities. I was determined my son would not have to do without any of the things I had to do without." He was driven by these compulsions even though he had, in fact, had a very comfortable childhood. Still, it seemed to him that he needed to tackle the world in some new way, because suddenly becoming a father had thrown him into an identity crisis.

After a new baby is born, parents find they have much less time for themselves and much less time for each other. Finances can become a problem, since expenses go up and income goes down — if one parent stops working outside the home. Almost every routine that provided structure is shattered. New routines have to be created, and many compromises have to be made. Even a couple's sex life changes drastically. At the same time, the mother discovers much of the doting attention that was paid to her when she was pregnant disappears, even though the interrupted and sleepless nights with a newborn can be more physically demanding than pregnancy was. In addition, the new parents are bombarded by unwanted advice and interference from parents, in-laws and well-meaning friends, who before the birth of the baby were happy to let them manage — or mismanage — their lives however they saw fit, but who now — for the sake of the baby — feel obliged to set them straight!

And, on top of all this, the new parents are instantly supposed to know — by instinct or by reading hundreds of conflicting theories on the subject — how to be parents. No wonder so many parents feel the stress is sometimes more than they can handle.

The less stress way

Simply being aware that the period after a child's birth is one of the most stressful in a marriage can help you survive it as a couple. Being flexible — going along smoothly with the new rhythms the baby introduces into your life — can also help a great deal. Many people are reassured by reading books about preparing for pregnancy and parenthood.

An uncooperative child creates a great deal more stress than a cooperative one. As your children get older, you can eliminate stress by creating an environment that helps them learn to be more cooperative and easier to get along with. Our experience has shown us that letting children know what we expect of them, explaining the consequences of their behavior to them and consistently following through with these consequences create the kind of environment cooperation flourishes in.

A framework for good discipline

Discipline, as we've described it in the use of consequences, isn't appropriate or needed until a child is more than one year old — Dr. Neifert says between eighteen months and two years of age — because until then a child cannot make the necessary connection between her actions and the effects of those actions. Still, we need to realize that we can begin building a framework for good discipline when a child is very young. As soon as a child begins to crawl, she is going to get her hands on things she shouldn't have. This is true even in the most carefully child-proofed homes, especially if there are older preschoolers with toys. When this happens you don't discipline her — she is just exploring and doesn't know she has done anything wrong — but you can begin to lay the groundwork for the kind of discipline you will establish later on. Between nine and twelve months a child begins to understand what a no-no is. When a child of this age gets a forbidden object into her hands, take it away, say no, and offer her an acceptable alternative plaything. If a child crawls too near a place you don't want her to be, gently but firmly pick her up, say, "No, you can't play here," and set her down in an acceptable place, saying, "Here's a good place to play." When your fourteen-month-old grabs the cat's tail, you can say, "No, that hurts the cat," then take her hand and show her how to gently touch the cat.

Dr. Kason and I believe that very young children understand a great deal more than adults sometimes give them credit for. But whether the child understands is not the issue here. What is important is that you are creating a certain kind of atmosphere; you are gently but firmly letting the child know there are some things she cannot have or do. At the same time you are building positive parenting habits.

In the examples above, you'll notice we suggest providing an alternative toy, place to play, or way of touching the cat. Much of what we do to reduce behavior that is not allowable in young children amounts to distracting their attention from the unacceptable and focusing it on the acceptable. This is an extremely important — and useful — fact for parents to recognize. Especially if they want to stay sane until their child reaches her third year!

Another important factor in building positive parenting habits is to begin, from birth on, to let your child know when she is doing the things that *are* acceptable or behaving in ways you like. It doesn't matter if she can't understand all the words you use, she will pick up on the warm, approving sounds in your voice. When your child plays nicely with a toy, praise her. When she entertains herself in her playpen while you're busy with something else, pause every once in a while to let her know how much you like what she's doing. Don't ignore her because you're afraid she might start crying for you if you remind her you're around — she might, but you can ignore it for minute, if you know there is nothing really wrong, and then focus on her when she is playing quietly again.

Keep expectations at the proper level

There are ways of introducing the idea of discipline to children as soon as they are crawling and toddling. The factor that is important here is your level of expectations. You can discipline an eight-month-old child by saying no and taking away a forbidden object, but you cannot expect her to understand or to actually learn not to touch that particular thing again. You can't expect a child younger than eighteen months to begin to grasp the idea that discipline is intended to change his behavior.

Children this young are not psychologically capable of a thought process like, "Mommy screamed at me last time I touched the cat food bowl, therefore I won't touch it again." If you smack a one-year-old, angrily grab an object from her or scream at her, you won't cause her to improve. You will only frighten her and cause her to think of you as a person who yells and smacks and grabs.

So while you shouldn't be afraid to begin to lay down the rudiments of firm, gentle discipline, you should not expect results. Because children develop mentally at vastly different rates — and have very different personalities — some toddlers will surprise you by catching on to what you mean and doing their best to comply. But you shouldn't *expect* it and you shouldn't get angry when they don't. Remember, they are not being "bad," they are only touching, tasting, smelling, prodding and tugging in order to explore and learn about the beautiful, bright shiny world they are discovering around them. They need to discover that it is a world they can trust.

As a child grows older she becomes increasingly able to grasp the concept of limits and understand the connection between breaking them and suffering the consequences. But while this process is going on, we need to remember that all parents and teachers sometimes fall short of their ideals of patience and understanding. We should not worry unnecessarily that our occasional shortcomings will harm our children as long as we use our reason and sincerely love and respect our children. Of course, we also need to be honest enough to seek help if we need it.

Facing the consequences

Hints on setting consequences

- Have a stockpile of appropriate consequences in your mind.
- There are many alternatives to spanking — and they work better.
- Remember, scolding is generally useless. Discuss. But don't overdue discussing and explaining.
- Never threaten.
- Set clear time limits for how long the consequence will last.
- Set a timer for things like time outs for children younger than five.
- Make consequences as immediate as possible.
- Keep your expectations at a proper level.

  ▮ Learn something about children's developmental stages so you know how much they really understand and how well they are able to comply.

  ▮ Don't expect the impossible of yourself. Remember that kids create stress. Don't be afraid to express your anger, feelings or needs in appropriate ways. This keeps things more honest and helps create a more positive atmosphere.

- Never humiliate a child; never cause her to lose face in front of others.
- Treat a child with respect even when you are carrying out consequences.

Consequences you can use

- Time outs (maximum one minute per year of age for kids younger than six).
  - In a chair away from the activity.
  - In another room.
  - In the child's bedroom.
  - In a chair facing the corner.
- Time outs where the child comes back when she is ready to behave.
- Take away the offending toy.
- Clean up, repair, or pay for mess or damage.
- Loss of privileges.
- Have children return things that don't belong to them.
- Apologize for misbehaviors.

Facing the consequences

Consequences you should never use

- ❏ Never cause bodily harm.
- ❏ Never do anything that would leave a mark on a child's skin.
- ❏ Never deprive a child of a need — use of the toilet, food, drink, sleep, warmth, love.
- ❏ Never lock a child into a confined or dark space such as a basement, attic or closet.
- ❏ Never lock a child out of the house or make her think he's been abandoned.
- ❏ Don't lock a child in her room — stand outside and hold the door if necessary.
- ❏ Don't ever threaten to use an inappropriate consequence.
- ❏ Don't use consequences that are harsher than the misbehavior calls for.

Guideline

Make sure consequences are fair, appropriate, and reasonable.

Chapter Five

A theory of hope

Positive reinforcement is one of the most effective child rearing techniques ever devised. It can be used by anyone who works or lives with children. The concept of positive reinforcement originated in a school of thought known as behavior modification. B.F. Skinner was one of the founders of this school. He took his ideas from scientists like Pavlov and developed a theory about how humans learn. The premise behind behavior modification is that people learn to do things — and their behavior is shaped — by the way they are rewarded. In a classic study done on behavior modification, children who sat quietly at their desks for a certain length of time were given a candy. It was found that when sitting quietly was rewarded, children developed the ability to sit quietly much more quickly than children who were not rewarded. They also learned to sit quietly for longer and longer lengths of time.

Behavior modification has its opponents. They point out that while behavior modification is effective in changing undesirable behavior, it does nothing to solve any underlying psychological need or problem that may have caused the misbehavior. Dr. Kason and I feel this criticism has some validity, and we're not strict behaviorists. Some of the techniques we discuss in this book, such as time outs, behavioral reward charts and contracting, have their roots in behavior modification theory. However, we prefer to use a combination of approaches in our work with children. We recognize that behavior modification can be effective and that it may be appropriate in many cases, especially on a specific problem behavior that cannot be improved by using the other approaches we suggest on their own. Still, Dr. Kason and I do not agree with the extremely structured sort of environment some behaviorists recommend. Nor do we think behavior modification should be the only, or the primary, tool a parent or teacher has at her command.

In classic behavior modification, desired behavior is rewarded and undesired behavior is either ignored or punished. The reward is known as positive reinforcement, and the punishment is called negative reinforcement. Dr. Kason and I try to emphasize the positive reinforcement aspect. Thus, the desirable and appropriate things a child does are rewarded, while the negative and inappropriate things he does are ignored, *whenever it is reasonable to do so.* Ignoring negative behavior is not being inconsistent. Limits are still set and consequences are still carried out when necessary.

Before we go further, we would also like to add the caution that parents or teachers should have a very thorough understanding of how to put the theory properly into practice before they begin to use it. In this chapter we give a description of positive reinforcement that should be adequate for most parents' and teachers' needs. More detailed information on classic behavior modification techniques can be found in the books by Patterson and Sloan. (See A Guide to Books on Parenting.)

Attention is a reward

Children, like adults, crave attention. They sometimes behave in certain ways just for the attention it brings them, and it is believed that much negative behavior comes about because a child gets some kind of satisfaction from the attention he gets when he is punished or when he is singled out in a group. In this sense, attention, regardless of whether it is negative or positive, is a reward. It might surprise you to think that a child — or a person of any age — would actually *want* to get negative attention. Although no healthy person prefers getting hit to getting hugged, it is essential to understand that human beings, especially children, need attention as desperately as they need food and water. Negative attention sometimes seems better than no attention at all.

Parents and teachers often focus most of their attention on the things a child does wrong rather on what he does right. A child can become aware of this at a subconscious level, and if he is in need of more attention he will often begin to increase his undesirable behavior. The use of positive reinforcement prevents — or breaks — this negative cycle by providing the child with the attention he needs when he does well. The idea is that if a child is getting a healthy amount of positive, loving attention he will not need to act in ways that will bring him negative forms of attention.

Positive reinforcement versus bribery

A common criticism made by people who misunderstand the concept of positive reinforcement is that it is a form of bribery. While both bribery and positive reinforcement do use some form of reward to influence behavior, it is our opinion that there are some important differences between the two. According to the dictionary, a bribe is a reward given in order to corrupt someone's actions or pervert a person's judgment. When using positive reinforcement a parent or teacher gives rewards in order to encourage a positive and desirable behavior — not to corrupt or pervert. The positive reinforcer is given while the child is still performing the desired behavior, or immediately after. A bribe is offered before the corrupt behavior takes place. A mobster, for instance, offers a judge money in order to have a certain charge dismissed when it comes before the courts. Some parents do use bribery with a child. They give the child a reward and extract a promise from him for future good behavior. The matter is further complicated by the fact that this type of reward almost always directly follows some type of *undesirable* behavior. The story of Larry, a good friend of mine, illustrates how parental bribery usually works. Larry's parents wanted very much for him to get good grades when he was in high school. When he received his first failing mark his father told him that he would give him five dollars if he promised never to do so poorly again. Larry took the money and agreed with good intentions. However, a connection had been made in his mind between doing poorly and receiving a reward. He continued to do poorly in school, and his father continued to "reward" him with larger and larger amounts of money each time he made a failing grade or got into some kind of trouble. The message was always the same: I'll give you this money if you promise not to do that again. In his last year of school, Larry got in trouble with the police. In desperation, his parents bought him a new car and made him promise to stay out of trouble. Of course, it didn't work. This process never succeeds, because the child receives the bribe right after a failure or misbehavior and makes a connection — often subconsciously — between the two.

An example of positive reinforcement

A description of how positive reinforcement works, on the other hand, can be seen in the case of Alisa, a girl I worked with. Alisa had a number of behavior problems, and although her difficulties were more extreme than those most parents encounter, her story provides an excellent example of how positive reinforcement can be used to change a specific, undesired behavior.

Several of Alisa's habits made it unpleasant for people to be around her. For example, she tended to yell rather than talk. I decided that this would be the specific behavior I would try to change with positive reinforcement. I began to refuse to respond to her whenever she yelled at me. I would, instead, wait until she said something in a quiet voice. As soon as she did this I immediately complimented her on her quiet way of speaking. Most times — but not every time — Alisa would speak quietly, I would let her know in some way that this was appropriate, desirable behavior that I felt she should strive to maintain. I would say things like, "It is nice to hear you talk quietly," or, "I really like the quiet way you're talking." Before Alisa had always received a great deal of attention when she was noisy in class. She was singled out by the teacher, or the attention of the entire class was focused upon her antics. Alisa, like all children, *needed* attention in order to thrive and survive. Therefore, an essential step in getting the positive reinforcement approach to work was to make sure the amount of attention she received for her negative — in this case noisy — behavior was eliminated, or at least greatly reduced. This was fairly easy. I steeled myself, gritted my teeth and did my best to ignore her when she yelled at me. Getting the other children to ignore the disruptions was not as easy, but it was not impossible. One of the tactics I used is one you might try as a teacher or a parent. Without humiliating or ostracizing Alisa in any way I said to the other children, "Kids, please don't give Alisa your attention when she does that. We're trying to help her get over wanting to disrupt the class." Because the other children didn't like Alisa's disruptive behavior and were made uncomfortable by it, they cooperated.

As soon as Alisa began to discover her noisy behavior wasn't getting her as much attention as her quiet behavior, she began to strive to speak more softly and cause fewer noisy disruptions. Each time Alisa reached a new plateau, I would stop rewarding her behavior at that level and would begin to focus my rewards on a slightly higher level of achievement. Thus, step by step, Alisa learned to speak more like the other children. Eventually, she stopped shouting in the classroom and speaking quietly became normal for her. As this happened, I gradually dropped all verbal rewards for quiet speech and accepted it as the norm. At the same time, I made absolutely sure that Alisa was getting plenty of positive attention for her work toward other goals.

Make positive responses a habit

In general, making positive responses should be a habit. We should be responding naturally in supportive ways — with smiles, encouraging words, and gentle touches — to the hundreds of sensitive, creative, and intelligent things every child does during the day. When this happens, the need for reprimands and punishment will be minimal. Unfortunately, if most of us give the matter some honest thought, we will discover that our children get the most attention from us when they behave negatively. We tend to focus on them much less when they behave well or succeed. It makes sense for us, as parents and teachers, to make sure we give our children the attention they need when they are doing the many marvelous things they do each day.

Positive reinforcement around the house

Let's take a look at how we can apply the principles of positive reinforcement to a child with a specific problem in the home. The step-by-step process is generally the same regardless of the behavior that needs to be improved. If the behavior problem seems very serious, you might want to see your family doctor to make sure there isn't some underlying medical, emotional or psychological cause. Next you'll need to consider the possibility that some basic need isn't being met. Say, for instance, your five-year-old is being very rough with his baby brother, who is just beginning to toddle. When you give the matter some thought you realize that your older child — let's call him Kevin — hasn't been getting nearly as much positive attention since the baby came along. In fact, you spend a lot of time yelling at him and telling him how *not* to handle the baby. In general, you are going to need to set aside more time for Kevin, perhaps a special time for each parent to be alone with him. You will also need to give him extra hugs and kisses during the day, and make more positive, loving comments about him and his behavior all the time. Your next step is to decide what positive behavior should replace the negative one. You need to be specific. Rather than thinking you want your child to be "better," you need to focus on definite behavior. Some of the individual elements that make up Kevin's rough behavior might include slapping the baby, jerking toys out of his hand, or pushing the baby roughly away when he comes near. Let's consider Kevin's slapping the baby as an example. You decide that the positive behavior you'd like to see replace this is gentle touching or caressing. Wait until the next time you see Kevin touch the baby in a gentle way, then you comment on it immediately, and give him the amount of attention you might have given him in the past when he hit the baby. Don't mention the times when he hit the baby; focus on what he's just done. You might say, "I really like it when you touch the baby like that." You might pick Kevin up, cuddle him for a minute and say, "It makes me happy when you rub the baby's head gently like that. I bet it makes him feel good, too." If Kevin never does caress the baby nicely, you would reward the behavior that comes closest to it, for instance, a fleeting gentle touch. As Kevin's behavior begins to improve, you stop rewarding these approximations of good behavior and reward only the actual desired behavior. This process is known as *shaping a behavior*.

Be sure that while you are placing more and more emphasis on the good behavior you are placing less on the bad. Ideally, you ignore the bad behavior altogether. In this case, of course, you could not possibly ignore the fact that Kevin is hitting his brother. But you do give it as little attention as possible. For instance, grab his hand in midair and say, "No! Hitting is not allowed!" Then return to whatever you were doing. If you need to establish a consequence for the behavior, that's fine, but it's better if you can make it one like a time out, so Kevin is out of the scope of your attention for a few minutes.

If Kevin's emotional needs are being met — and if there are no underlying psychological or medical problems — you may be surprised at how quickly he begins to handle the baby gently.

Regardless of the type of behavior you're trying to change, you need to remember that if the child's behavior is nowhere near the ultimate goal in the beginning, you reward the closest he comes to it. Although the changes the child makes may seem small or insignificant to the adult, they may seem like a big improvement to the child, and he will be able to move to the next stage as he gains confidence. Then, as soon as the level you are praising becomes fairly standard, you begin to focus your positive comments on the next level the child is able to attain.

Positive reinforcement and school problems

Many teachers use positive reinforcement in their work. Parents can also help a child who is doing poorly in school by focusing on the positive aspects of the child's work. They can begin by praising any piece of work the child brings home that has a slightly improved grade. If the grades on all the child's papers are unsatisfactory the parent can point out parts that look good — even the slightest improvement can be remarked upon. When a paper with a better grade or a report card with higher marks is finally brought home the parents need to spend as much time praising it as they would have spent, in the past, criticizing it. This is an essential point. Often parents spend a great deal of time scolding or punishing the child for his poor marks and admonishing him to do better. This has a negative effect. The child becomes doubtful about his ability and discouraged about the possibility of improving. He hears his parents tell him how bad he has been, and feeling bad or stupid lingers in his mind. The child is receiving a great deal of attention during the scolding process. He is singled out from the other children; he is talked to extensively, and he receives the undivided attention of his mother and father. His parents, in short, show their concern. Because of the hectic life-style prevalent in North America today, in some families this is the most attention a child ever receives from his parents. It is important to keep in mind the fact that the child is probably not *intentionally* failing in order to get attention. In his conscious mind he may well be berating himself constantly and thinking about how much he wants to do better so his parents will love him more. At some level in his subconscious mind, however, he has made the connection between failure and receiving the attention he craves.

Due to the tremendous stress placed on academic success, a child who is a failure in school is almost certain to get a lot of attention. Although all failure is not caused by a need for attention, many of today's foremost educators say that this is the motivating factor in a surprising number of cases. Positive reinforcement is the key to helping a child overcome his difficulties. Even when the need for attention is not the main factor in school failure, positive reinforcement can be a powerful tool in helping a child improve his concept of himself, and consequently his school performance. We deal with this in more detail in Chapter Thirteen.

Praise must be sincere

It is imperative that the person who praises the child is sincere. It is not necessary that the child be rewarded every time he does well, but the praise should always be simple, warm and honest. Remember: even if a child's work or behavior is not as good as the work of his peers, if it's the best he's ever done, it represents excellent work for him, and he deserves to hear it. If the work or behavior is good, but not as good as you feel he could do, tell him this, too, but remember to emphasize the good! By applying this process to any negative behavior a parent can do a tremendous amount to help his child improve.

Some children, and all children in certain situations, respond more readily to concrete rewards. In other words, they work toward their goals better when, in addition to praise, they receive gold stars, happy-face stickers, tokens that can be traded in for certain privileges, or a prize of some sort. We cover this concept in more detail in Chapter Six, when we discuss behavioral reward charts.

A cry for attention

When a child can't verbalize his feelings, he sometimes tells us with his actions. When a child stops listening to warnings or ignores punishment, it often means he needs more positive attention. A father once came to me and said he was punishing his eight-year-old son frequently, but that no form of punishment was effective in curbing the child's increasingly disturbing behavior. This situation had progressed to the point that the child, John, kept wading along the edge of a dangerous creek near his home even though he had been punished for it several times.

In order to begin to correct this behavior, the father had to consider how much attention John received during the day, how much of it was positive and how much of it was scolding and punishment. The father admitted that because John's behavior was so distressing, the child was continually being warned, scolded, or punished. This had become the predominant kind of attention John was receiving, and it had lost its meaning. In fact, punishment was having quite the opposite effect of what it was intended to have and John was purposely behaving negatively in order to get the attention he craved.

The father was determined to improve the situation. He began to spend time each day complimenting John for his good behavior. He made a special effort to notice all the fine things John was doing, no matter how small they were, for he began to realize these things did not seem small to the child. He complimented the boy's coloring, he acknowledged the helpful things John did around the house, and he made a point of commenting on how John was staying away from the stream. When the father felt it was absolutely necessary to punish John, he made efforts to think in terms of appropriate consequences, rather than handing out random types of punishment. And, as he increased the amount of positive attention he gave his son, he found that the times he needed to use consequences decreased.

Positive reinforcement is a theory of hope. A great deal of failure and negative behavior can be transformed into success and acceptable behavior by praising the positive and building on the abilities children have. This is how to help them develop into loving, confident adults.

Using positive reinforcement

❑ Positive reinforcement works — children learn to behave in ways that are rewarded.

❑ Be careful — both positive and negative attention can be rewards.

❑ Give children lots of love, affection and attention — respond to the wonderful things they do.

❑ How to use positive reinforcement.

■ Choose a reward that really pleases the child.

■ Give the reward *immediately* after the desired behavior. (If it's a behavior that stretches over a period of time you can reward during and after.)

■ Ignore bad behavior if you can, or give appropriate consequences.

■ If the child never performs the desired behavior, shape the child's behaviour by rewarding the closest thing to the behavior you desire.

■ Each time the child reaches a new level, stop rewarding that level of behavior and begin to reward a higher one — go on until the goal is reached.

■ Even after goals are reached, make sure the child gets all the positive attention he needs.

Guideline

Kids need a tremendous amount of attention. Make sure they get it for the positive — not the negative — things they do.

Chapter Six

What to do when "don't" doesn't work

Walk through any busy place where parents and children are together, like a park or a supermarket, and you will see how often children refuse to listen to the word *don't*. For parents, this is, at best, annoying and, at worst, tragic. When a child doesn't listen to "Don't get dirty," it doesn't matter much; when she doesn't listen to "Don't run in the road!" it can matter a great deal.

Children block out the word *don't* for a variety of reasons. One of the most common is that the child has learned, through experience, that nothing will happen to her when she ignores what her parents tell her not to do. Saying *don't* is, in effect, setting a limit — and when a limit is broken a consequence

What to do when "don't" doesn't work

needs to be carried out. As we have mentioned, it is extremely easy for a child to develop a nonchalant attitude toward the word *don't* when nothing ever happens when she *does*. Although this may sound obvious, Dr. Kason and I cannot count the hundreds of times we have heard an adult tell a child firmly not to do something, watched the child do it, then noticed that the adult made no attempt to interrupt the child or to carry out an appropriate consequence afterward. These kids learn early on that *don't* doesn't mean a thing.

Children will also ignore *don't* when it is overused. I saw a clear example of this — and how serious it could be — a few years ago at a picnic. Throughout the afternoon I noticed that one particular father was extremely concerned with the behavior of Sarah, his five-year-old daughter. Every time I was near the father I heard him tell Sarah not to do something. "Don't bounce that ball over here!" "Don't eat so many marshmallows!" "Don't get your blouse dirty!" and "Don't bother me!" These were just a few commands I heard in one fifteen-minute period.

Later that afternoon I heard the father yell, "Don't climb that tree!" and saw him run toward Sarah, who was hugging the trunk of a precarious-looking young maple. I was not surprised to see her scurry up the tree in spite of the father's frantic warnings. By the time the father reached the tree, Sarah was well into the unsturdy branches. It was almost pathetic to watch the father stand by the trunk and continue to yell like a broken record, "Don't climb that tree," while his daughter went higher and higher.

Situations like this occur when a child is restricted at every turn, particularly when many of the restrictions are ridiculous — like telling a child not to get her shirt dirty at a picnic! Or when every restriction, regardless of importance, is given in the same tone of voice. When statements like "Don't wrinkle your dress" and "Don't touch the stove" are expressed in the same way, the significance of the more serious command is lost to the child.

There is nothing wrong with telling children what they must not do, but they will listen to *don't* much more readily when the word is used sparingly. If Sarah had not been told what *not* to do all day long, she may well have listened when her father told her not to climb the tree. A parent or teacher can create a secure and structured environment without restricting the child to the point where she becomes rebellious.

Emphasize what the child may do

One of the most effective ways of doing this is to emphasize what the child may do rather than what she may not do and, at the same time, to offer her an acceptable alternative. With a little effort an enterprising adult can usually find the right words. For instance, instead of yelling, "Don't bounce that ball over here!" Sarah's father might have said, "You can't bounce the ball here." He could then have explained the reason for the restriction and suggested an alternative: "The ball could hit the baby here. But you can bounce it over by the trees or over there where the big kids are playing." Sarah would probably have accepted one of those alternatives. If she had acted like she was going to bounce the ball again near the baby, her father could then have explained what the consequence would be and offered another alternative: "Sarah, if you bounce the ball here, I will take it away for an hour. Do you want to sit here with me and play quietly or do want to go over there and play with the ball?"

It's certainly quicker to yell *don't* than to spend time explaining the reasons a child can't do something and suggesting alternatives to her. However, if the parent or teacher takes the time to explain whenever he can, he will find that the child listens to *don't* when it is really important. Amy was a three-year-old I took care of a few days every week, and she taught me this lesson. Amy's parents had made a sincere effort to create a well-structured yet open environment for her. The limits they set were clear, and consequences were consistently carried out. They explained their reasons for limits and offered positive alternatives whenever they could. She rarely heard them say don't, and when they did they meant it. One of the important *don'ts* in Amy's life was in regard to a nest of poisonous spiders that lived near the back of the garage and seemed to return each time they were thought to be exterminated.

Although I was worried about letting her play in the backyard while she was under my care, her parents insisted that she would not go near the spiders because she had been told not to do so. The limit had been clearly set, and what Amy *could* do had been emphasized. She could ride her trike; she could play on the swings or on the slide or in the sandbox; she could go anywhere in the backyard she liked except by the garage where the spiders were. Being quite skeptical that a three-year-old would follow such instructions, I watched her carefully for several days as she played in the backyard. Even though Amy was a fearless child, she never once approached the spiders. On two or three occasions she did, however, come into the house and ask me to take her to see the spiders. This, of course, I did, holding her by the hand and explaining to her simple facts about the spiders and how they lived.

It is up to a parent or another adult who knows a child well to determine, in a responsible manner, where she can play and what she can be trusted to do. Of course, whenever possible, it is better to remove the threat of danger than to set a limit against it.

Provide opportunities for expression

If we consider the occasions we tell a child not to do something, we will see that the majority of them do not have to do with safety. Rather they are related to creating what we think of as messes or to expressing anger. At other times the child is exhibiting curiosity and a desire to explore the environment. All these activities are natural urges found in every healthy child; they are, in fact, *needs*. It stands to reason that the child who is given ample opportunity to explore or make a mess in appropriate situations will have less need to do these things at inappropriate times and places. Dr. Kason and I have found that when an environment is structured so that children have enough freedom to express their anger, make messes, and satisfy their curiosity, the number of times *don't* has to be used is greatly diminished.

The first time I saw this principle at work was when my sister's son, Jeff, was two years old. Jeff, like all toddlers, loved to imitate his parents. At one point my sister found she could barely work in her kitchen because of Jeff's enthusiastic exploration of her cupboards. Tiring of telling him not to remove things from the cupboards and realizing that he learned a great deal from his explorations, she tried out a solution: She took one cupboard and one drawer that Jeff could easily reach and filled them with old pots and pans, unbreakable bowls, large wooden spoons, brightly colored plastic measuring cups, and other harmless, but interesting, kitchen gadgets. These became Jeff's cupboard, drawer and dishes; he was allowed to play with them as he liked.

Jeff rattled and banged in uninterrupted glee. When he did approach his mother's cupboards and drawers, she would simply remind him that he could play with the things in his cupboard but not with the things in hers. This worked far better than having to say "Don't touch that!" again and again.

Other parents have expanded on this idea and created toolboxes and workbenches full of harmless equipment for their children. One couple who was distressed by their son's decided interest in their expensive stereo system found some relief by obtaining an inexpensive, used system for the boy and giving him some of their old albums along with several children's albums he liked.

It's great to make a mess

Kids don't just *like* to get dirty and make messes, they *need* to. It's one of the few ways they can express their emotions and satisfy their curiosity at the same time. If you've ever watched a three-year-old making mud pies, you'll have noticed how she smears the mud around with her hands, smells it, rubs it against her skin, and tries to taste it once in a while. She'll shape it into something that vaguely looks like a pie. And then what? She'll smash it! She'll beat it into absolute nothingness with her little toy spatula or her hands. Then she'll start the whole process over again. This is a wonderful example of how children, by mucking around, can explore their environment and vent their frustrations. Expressing anger and venting frustrations are sometimes the most important function of noisy and messy play.

No one, of course, wants anything as gunky as mud in the middle of their home or classroom. Although some day-care centres have indoor sandboxes, most homes don't have anywhere a child can make a mess when it's too cold to go outside. Playing with water can be an excellent alternative. A child can spend hours sitting on a plastic sheet on the kitchen floor with a couple of bowls of soapy water, cups for dipping, and a few containers to pour the water in. As soon as my goddaughters were old enough to stand safely by themselves on a chair and reach the kitchen sink, they were splashing in water at my house. I have always been amazed at how long they can entertain themselves with this activity. Pouring warm, sudsy water from cup to cup, splashing, making bubbles, and sponging up the spills seem to satisfy something deep and basic in their natures.

A teacher I once worked with lived in a tiny house with her husband and daughter, Leslie. The girl's bedroom was very small; she had no place of her own to play and often turned their minuscule living room into a disaster area. The mother, however, was able to find an alternative to continually curbing Leslie's activities. She set aside a corner of the kitchen with a small table and chair, covered the walls behind it with poster board, and spread the floor under it with a plastic sheet. Next, she equipped the area with crayons, paste, finger paints, watercolors, markers, bubbles, and so on, etc. This was "Leslie's place," and she could experiment, splash around, mark on the poster board, and make messes to her heart's content.

Having a spot like this made it easier for the child to keep her play in the living room organized, and it also gave her a place for unhampered creative expression. In the event that Leslie would try, as most four-year-olds do, to use crayons on the living-room walls, her mother could say, "Leslie, you cannot mark on the walls. If you want to color something big, you can use the poster in your play area. What do you want to do? Stay here and color in a book or go to your poster and color there?"

This type of logic is surprisingly well understood by even very young children and, given the opportunity, they will often make good decisions. Giving a child her own equipment or drawer does not necessarily mean she will always prefer her own things over the adult's. It does, however, help satisfy some of her basic needs, and it can eliminate many negative situations. Parents also need to remember that children need plenty of opportunity to run, jump, and shout so that they can burn off their excess energy in appropriate ways. Too much pent-up energy invariably results in misbehaviour.

Alternatives to limits and consequences
Modeling

Limits and consequences are the foundation of good discipline, but they can be overused. Just as a child will turn off her ears when she hears the word *don't* too often, she will begin to stop paying attention when there are too many limits or when consequences are handed out too often. There are, however, other ways to encourage good behavior. One of the most important of these is called modeling. We've all noticed that children learn — particularly at certain stages — by copying or imitating the behavior of the important adults in their lives. As my grandmother used to say, "Monkey see, monkey do."

Most adults know that children tend to pick up bad habits, so they make an effort to set a good example in certain situations, for instance, by using good manners and not swearing in front of the children. But children learn from adult behavior *all* the time. They do not understand the meaning of the saying, "do as I say, not as I do." They are confused when they get scolded for imitating their parents. A child doesn't understand why she can't slap her little brother if that's the way she sees her mother and father treating him all the time.

Adults can teach — or encourage — a child to behave in a particular positive way by behaving that way themselves. When a friend of mine wanted to teach her three-year-old son how to treat their new puppy, she sat on the floor beside it and stroked it gently until her son came over and started to imitate her. Later when the boy grabbed at the puppy's tail she stroked the puppy again and said, "Remember. This is the way we touch the puppy. Softly. Gently."

One afternoon, in an educational clinic for problem children where I was working, some six-year-olds were playing school at break time. The boy who was playing teacher was correcting imaginary assignments, and was saying, "Excellent work!" to one girl, and, "Good printing!" to another. Not long after that I had the opportunity of watching a different group of children play school. The girl who was leading the class was saying, "Don't let me hear another sound out of you!" and, "This paper is a mess — do it again!" The two children had modeled their behavior on their teachers, with strikingly different results.

Explaining expectations and reasons

Children also learn about proper behavior when parents and teachers take the time to explain their expectations to them and discuss the reasons something should be done. Some people believe that when this is done properly it is the only disciplinary technique ever needed. For some children this works all the time, and for most, it works some of the time. A child learns more from a parent who says, "Those rocks are too high for you climb. You could fall and get hurt — you can climb over here where it's safe," than from one who just yells, "Don't do that."

Even very young children can benefit from hearing reasons and explanations. When a toddler has her plate precariously balanced on the edge of the table, her father might move it back and say, "Plates need to be away from the edge. If they're not, they fall." Eventually the child begins to understand. Kids become proud of knowing how and why things should be done correctly. The other day my five-year-old goddaughter started to lick the butter knife at the dinner table, but then stopped herself, knife in midair, and said proudly, "You shouldn't lick the butter knife and put it back in the butter, 'cause you'll get *germs* on the butter!" One of her parents had obviously been explaining some of the reasons behind good table manners.

When a parent or teacher uses reasoning as a way of improving a particular negative behavior, he should first clearly describe the behavior, then say how it makes him feel and why it makes him feel that way. Next, he should clearly state the *expected* behavior. For example, if your six-year-old throws her wet bathing suit on her bed when she comes home from her swimming lesson, you could say, "When you throw your suit on the bed, it makes me angry because the sheets get wet, and then I have to change the sheets. Your suit needs to be hung up in the bathroom as soon as you come home." Notice that when you use this method, you get your point across without falling into the trap of labeling your child or judging her behavior. When we label and judge we say things like, "You're such a slob," or, "You never think about the work you make for me!" or, "Can't you ever do anything right?"

One caution when you are explaining expectations and reasons: keep your explanations short and age-appropriate. Kids tend to tune out when adults go on and on.

Behavior modification techniques
Charts

Many parents and teachers have found a behavior modification chart to be a real lifesaver for correcting a negative behavior that seems be getting out of hand or for encouraging an important new habit. The first step in making one of these charts is for the adult and child to sit down together and discuss the behavior that needs to be improved or attained. These are the child's goals. If a long-term goal is involved it should be broken down into easily attained short-term goals. These, in turn, should be divided into specific, concrete tasks. The tasks must be things the child is capable of accomplishing. Next, the adult and child agree on an appropriate reward for performing each of these tasks each day. Then they draw up the chart together. Tasks are listed on the left-hand side and the days of the week across the top; lines are drawn across and down to make boxes.

Behavior modification charts are often used to encourage a child to do household chores. Specific tasks might be, "Make the bed every day," "Empty the garbage every day," "Do dishes two times per week," and, "Sweep kitchen two times per week." The reward might be that the child earns 25¢ of her $3.50 weekly allowance for every task she completes. Thus, if she does all her tasks, she gets her whole allowance. As soon as she completes a task she gets to make a check mark or put a sticker on the chart in the appropriate box. The parent makes a point of remarking on each sticker that goes up and praising the child for her accomplishments.

At a specified time at the end of the week, parent and child sit down together again and count up the check marks or stickers. The parent fulfills his end of the bargain by giving the child the appropriate amount of money, praising the child on her progress and giving her a good deal of positive attention. The adult does *not* criticize the child for the chores that were not done. Neither does he give the child any more money than she has earned — even if she pleads or promises to do better.

The reward doesn't necessarily have to be allowance money, but it does have to be something the child really wants, like points or tokens that can be traded for something like permission to go to movie on Saturday night or to use the family car. With younger children sometimes just getting a sticker or star — and the recognition that goes with it — is enough.

A behavior modification chart won't work if the reward isn't something the child really cares about having. It will also usually fail if the child doesn't get recognition for her accomplishments regularly. Further, what she has earned is hers: it cannot be taken away from her as punishment for some other misbehavior. The chart is a contract between a child and an adult. The two strike a bargain — and both must live up to their ends of the deal.

Contracting

Some children prefer to have a contract which is written down on a sheet of paper. This is known as contracting and has become very popular with parents and teachers. The contract needs to state clearly what each person expects of the other: "I will remember to feed and walk the dog every night this week. Each time I do my dad will give me fifty cents." Contracts can be more elaborate and include a number of expectations, some earning more valuable rewards than others. They can also contain both long- and short-term goals. However, the goals need to be specific. It also has to be easy to determine whether the goal has been reached, and there should be a place on the contract where progress can be recorded. Time limits also need to be clearly stated. Once the contract is drawn up, both the adult and child sign it. Here's an example:

"Every night I completely finish my math homework I will receive one check mark on my contract chart. When I have five check marks, my parents will allow me to go to the show on Saturday night. My goal is to earn five check marks this week, so I can go the show with Sarah this Saturday night. If I have no math homework, I can earn my check mark by reviewing my math with one parent for twenty minutes.

Signed: Joan Johnson and Frederick Johnson."

A contract is a *mutual* agreement; both parties have to feel comfortable with the goals and rewards and both have to live up to their ends of the bargain. The adult may need to agree to change his behavior. For instance, when Joan and her father discussed their contract, Joan might have said that it bothered her when her father nagged her about doing her math homework. During the discussion, Joan might have explained that she was already nervous about math because she was having trouble with it, and that her father's attitude made her more uptight. In this case, a clause could have been added to the contract stating that Joan's father would agree to trust her to do her math and earn her check mark on her own. If the father forgot and nagged about math, he would have to put twenty-five cents in a kitty. All the money in the kitty would be added to Joan's allowance at the end of the week.

Once the contract was drawn up and signed, Joan and her father would need to agree on a specific time — perhaps Friday night after dinner — when they would sit down and discuss the week's progress and revise and improve the contract for the next week, if necessary.

The adult involved must remember that the child's progress needs to be recognized not just by material rewards set down in the contract but also with praise, attention, and positive comments. The idea behind the use of contracts — or charts — is not to *train* a child to do things, but to help her see that meeting goals and fulfilling obligations are valuable experiences in themselves, and that they make a person feel good about herself.

Treats

Structuring an activity or a period of time so the child earns a treat by accomplishing something or behaving in a certain manner is a technique that often eliminates the need for discipline. As I mentioned earlier, at the clinic I worked in, each hour-long tutoring session was broken into forty-five minutes of work time and fifteen minutes of free time. At the beginning of the session the child and teacher would discuss and agree on what could reasonably be accomplished in the time frame. The child earned her free time by working steadily and accomplishing her goals. As she worked the teacher would praise her efforts. If she began to misbehave or ignore her work, the teacher would remind her that she was working toward getting her free time: "I know you're looking forward to playing with the Transformers during your free time. Let's get back to work." If the child continued to waste time she would have to work during her free time until her assignment was done. The adult must emphasize that the child earns the treat with her good behavior or hard work — the adult doesn't punish her by taking it away when she doesn't do well enough.

Almost any activity can be made to run more smoothly using this concept. When my goddaughters were four and five-and-a-half years old, I began taking them swimming during the winter at an indoor pool. On one occasion, I noticed they were getting overly excited and not listening when I reminded them not to run on wet tiles and to follow the other pool rules. The next time we went, as we walked by the snack bar, I mentioned that the gingerbread men looked good and I would like to get them each one after we were through swimming. Then I explained that the gingerbread men would be their reward for following all the pool rules. We went over the rules together. During the swim I gave them a gentle reminder about the rules — and the reward they were trying to earn — each time I thought they needed it. From time to time I complimented them on their good behavior and on how well they were following the rules. There was not a single problem the entire time they were in the water. As soon as they finished swimming and getting dressed we went to the snack bar, and I bought them their treats, again commenting on how pleased I had been with their behavior. Both girls were much more excited about the gingerbread than they normally would have been about having a cookie. They were quite proud to have earned their rewards.

Meeting basic needs

Whenever a child — particularly a preschooler — is disobedient or cranky, we should check to be sure her basic needs are being met. Could she be hungry, tired or too hot? Could her clothes be uncomfortable or wet? Could she be ill? If so, it is the problem that needs to be corrected — not her misbehavior. Instead of scolding a child who is temperamental because dinner is late, a parent can say something like, "Dinner's late and you're *really* hungry. I'm getting it ready as quick as I can. Why don't you have a cracker while you wait?" or, "No wonder you're cranky. You're very hungry! We'll fix that in just a minute."

Children whose basic needs aren't being met tend to disobey a great deal. Any teacher can tell you that the most difficult children are often those who come to school without having enough food or sleep or proper clothing. Although it's easy for most of us to understand that these children are angry and frustrated because they aren't getting what they need, we often forget that even children who are well clothed and fed can become angry and frustrated if they are not getting enough attention.

The kind of attention a child needs can take many forms: physical affection, praise and recognition, the amount of time her parents spend with her. Some parents, for instance, give their children plenty of praise and encouragement when they see them, but they don't see them enough. Others talk to their children a great deal, but never hug them or hold them enough. Still others aren't aware they give one child far more attention than another.

A great deal of disobedience and temperamental behavior disappears when *all* a child's basic needs are met.

Praise

Occasionally parents and teachers find that the praise they give their children isn't having the effect they want or expect. They may be using positive words like "great," "terrific," "fabulous" or "very good," and yet find that the children react to the praise in a negative way, for instance, by seeming to disbelieve it or by becoming anxious. Other children, in spite of the praise, may still seem to lack self-confidence or have low self-esteem.

If this is happening to your child, the Adlerian concept that praise works better when it *describes* rather than *evaluates* might help you remedy the situation. You are *evaluating* when your six-year-old daughter brings you a drawing of a butterfly and you say, "That's great!" You are *describing* when you say, "I really like the colors you chose! The yellow and orange are very bright. It makes me happy just to look at that picture." You are telling the child in a concrete way both what you like about the picture and how it makes you feel. Adlerian psychologists, particularly those influenced by Dr. Haim Ginnott, tell us that when an adult gives praise by describing in an appreciative way what he sees or feels, the child is able to follow through and praise *herself*. Thus, the girl who drew the butterfly might, after her parent had finished talking about the picture, say, "Gee, I'm good at choosing colors. I think I'll make a really bright flower now!"

Another technique for using this concept is to sum up, in a positive word or two, what the child has done. Say, for instance, you walk into your son's room and find he has done a very good cleaning job. Instead of saying, "You're a good boy for cleaning your room," you might say, "I see a shining floor, clothes that are hung up neatly in the closet, toys that are all put away. I call that *thorough cleaning!*"

Adlerians are concerned with the issue of a child's self-esteem. They feel that it is not a good idea to tell a child she is good when she cleans her room, because she might feel she's bad when she doesn't clean it. They point out that cleaning a room has nothing to do with goodness or badness — it has to do with cleaning! They feel that praise should focus on a child's *strengths* and what is *right* about her, and that it should help the child discover for herself that she does have these positive characteristics. To use this method the way Adlerians recommend, you must phrase much of your speech to your children in a specific manner. Some people find this fairly natural and have good results. Other people find they don't feel comfortable with the necessary patterns of speech, or they think this specific way of talking doesn't seem to fit their personalities or parenting style. If you would like to learn more about Ginott's ideas about praise or the Adlerians' ideas on communicating effectively with children, see the reading list at the back of the book.

Dr. Kason and I use evaluative terms like "good," "terrific," and "wonderful" when telling a child what we think of her and her behavior. We say things like, "You're one terrific kid!" "That's a wonderful drawing!" "I think you are a very good girl!" all the time in our dealings with children. But we also use a lot of descriptive praise. In general, we try not to worry too much about wording our conversation with children in any particular way as long as the positive message is clear.

We have found, however, that praise is more effective and better appreciated when a few points are kept in mind. First, be sincere. Find something you like and point it out. Second, never overdo it. A child feels like she can't live up to expectations that are too high. Third, focus on specifics whenever you can. In other words, point out what the child has accomplished: "I think you did a very good job cleaning your room. The floor is shining." "This printing shows real improvement. The margins are straight and I can read every word!" This is especially important when you're helping a child learn a new skill: "Good swimming! You've got the flutter kick down, and your arms are almost straight." Fourth, tell kids when they are helpful: "Thanks for setting the table. I'm rushed tonight and that really helps." "I really appreciated the way you put your game away. The living room looks great." Fifth, never make a reference to past failures or mistakes when you praise. In other words, say: "This report card shows a big improvement!" Don't say: "These grades are a lot better than all the bad ones you brought home last time."

Never forget that kids are different

As we mentioned in Chapter Three, individual children need varying amounts of structure and respond differently to disciplinary techniques. One reason for differences in children within the same family is the order in which they were born. Although it is beyond the scope of this book to describe all the problems associated with birth order, it's important to mention a couple that are often directly related to misbehavior. It is quite common, for instance, for a child to act out when a new baby is born. This is usually most pronounced when the second child is born. The first child suddenly finds she has to share her parent's attention, and she will inevitably feel some degree of jealousy. She may strive to increase the amount of attention she receives by misbehaving or by regressing — falling back into behavior patterns she has long since outgrown. She may, for instance, want a bottle again, wet her pants, or throw tantrums. Parents can minimize these difficulties by focussing as much attention as possible on the first child, spending time alone with her, involving her with the care of the new baby and helping her to feel special because she is able to assist. This process generally needs to be repeated — especially for the youngest child in the family — each time a new baby is born.

Another common problem related to birth order is the middle child syndrome. This child sometimes feels a lack of identity or recognition in the family. The oldest child is able to *do* more and is given more privileges. The youngest child is the baby of the family and usually gets attention. This leaves the middle child wondering what could possibly make her special. If she doesn't find some way to stand out — by having some special ability or excelling at a particular activity — she will often use negative behavior to get attention. Parents can prevent this by recognizing the middle child's need to feel important within the family, by giving her individual attention, and by avoiding comparisons among siblings. They can also build her self-esteem by helping her discover her own unique qualities.

Birth order is one of the many factors that make kids behave in different ways. A colleague of Dr. Kason's, a family physician and the mother of four children, told Dr. Kason a story that exemplifies how different children react to limits and consequences — in fact, to everything a parent does.

One day the mother had taken three of her children and two of their friends to choir practice at their church. On their way out, the children saw a tray full of doughnuts on a table in one of the meeting rooms. The children realized the doughnuts must have been set out for a special meeting, but they went into the room and each took one anyway. When they got to the car, the kids were still munching on the doughnuts. The mother asked where they had gotten them, and when she heard the story she told the children they had to go back into the church, apologize, and offer to pay for the doughnuts out of their allowance money.

The children all did as they were told, but later the mother discovered each child had had a profoundly different reaction. Three of the children — one of hers and the two friends — simply did as they were asked. The episode was then, as far as these three were concerned, completely finished. Another of her children, however, was quite angry when he came back from apologizing. He said, "Mom, I don't think that consequence was fair. What we did wasn't that bad — because it wasn't really stealing — and we shouldn't have had to apologize like that." The reaction of the remaining child didn't become apparent until later that evening, when she came into the living room sobbing and saying she had to talk to her mother. She explained, through her tears and anguish, how terrible she felt about taking the doughnut. She said she had known it was wrong all along, and had felt bad about herself because she hadn't had the courage to stand up to the others or do what she thought was right. The mother and daughter had a two-hour discussion — only then did the girl feel better.

This story illustrates how very differently children, even brothers and sisters, think and respond. Since what works with one child doesn't necessarily work with another, parents and teachers need to be sensitive to children's differences and flexible enough to deal with each child in the most effective way possible. The story should also remind us that each child is a person. She is more than the sum of what she has learned and inherited from her parents. Thus she brings to life — and to every discipline situation — a unique self, which has good and bad traits, strengths and weaknesses that are hers alone. This means that some parents do a lot of things wrong and still manage to raise good kids. Other parents do the right things and have kids with problems. Ultimately, no parent can take all the blame — or all the credit — for the way a child develops.

When "don't" doesn't work

- Avoid overusing the word don't.
- Make sure you mean it when you say *don't* — set and follow through with consequences.
- Emphasize what the child may do.
- Demonstrate good behavior. It's hard for a child to "do as you say, not as you do."
- Explain the reason for your limits and expectations — but don't overdo it.
- Try a behavior reward chart for difficult problems.
- Try contracting for difficult problems with older kids.
- Arrange it so that the child can earn treats by behaving well during potentially troublesome activities.
- Be sure the child's needs are met — don't forget the need for attention.
- Help build the child's self-esteem with praise that's specific, descriptive, and sincere.

Guideline

Make sure the child has plenty of opportunity to express anger, get dirty, make messes, explore the environment and burn up energy.

Chapter Seven

Love never spoiled a child

Children are not spoiled by love. Spoiling is a process that occurs when a child lives in an environment of inconsistency and inappropriately placed attention.

Scores of the children I have worked with have been called spoiled, but I have noticed these children are the ones who don't have a clear idea what their limits are. They tend to be treated with kindness one day and unpredictable anger the next, or their misbehavior is ignored one day and punished severely the next. They are simply not the children who have been overly cuddled, held, and kissed as babies or comforted, supported, and accepted as youngsters. They are also not necessarily the children who have been given excessive material gifts.

Even though most people are probably in fairly close agreement about what the word spoiled means, we would like to give you our definition. To us, a spoiled child is one who throws tantrums, who lashes out in anger every time he does not get his own way, and who "bosses" his parents, other adults and children, confidently believing that he will be obeyed. A spoiled child does not tolerate the word "no" or even the words "wait" or "later." He screams, yells, kicks, bites, whines, and shouts insults, thoroughly *expecting* that his behavior will manipulate the adult in charge into giving him what he wants.

Over the years, Dr. Kason and I have made a connection between the inconsistency with which children like this have been handled and the fact that they seemed to be spoiled. We feel these children become selfish, demanding, and controlling in a vain attempt to bring some sort of order to their uncertain world.

A demanding child

Inconsistency was a pattern in the upbringing of the first spoiled child I encountered. I was a six-year-old child myself at the time and had gone for a visit with my mother to the home of a new neighbor. I remember watching Sherry, who was about four years old, pick up a knife and brandish it at her mother during a temper tantrum. Sherry's mother pleaded with her never to do such a terrible thing again, then gave in to to the demands Sherry had been making during her tantrum. After we left I asked my mother why Sherry had not gotten a spanking. She replied that

Sherry was spoiled and her mother never spanked her. I wondered at the time why a kid who was lucky enough to never get spanked would want to run after her mother with a knife. It did not take me long to figure it out. I noticed that Sherry's mother sometimes allowed her to do as she pleased, sometimes screamed horribly at her, sometimes sent her to her room. Every time we visited Sherry's I felt insecure and unsettled. Even though I thought Sherry's mother was a nice lady, I did not like being there.

Later, when I heard people say things like, "Don't pick up the baby, it will spoil him," I became confused. Sherry's mother had never picked her up that I could recall; in fact, she usually ignored her. The memory of my experience with Sherry never left me. Years later, when I began to work in clinical settings with children who were so "spoiled" their parents had to seek professional help, I began to notice how inconsistent these parents were with their children. It also became clear that these unwitting parents had been reinforcing their children's negative behavior by giving in to their demands — they were actually teaching their children to become more demanding.

Children learn to throw tantrums

All children try to get something they want by throwing tantrums at one time or another. This is a normal developmental behavior that most children experiment with sometime between the ages of eighteen and twenty-four months. The wise parent puts an end to this undesirable behavior by ignoring it whenever possible. If one of your children is throwing tantrums, you probably need to ignore the tantrum. As long as your child is safe from harm, you can walk away or turn your back on him while he is yelling and kicking. If there is any possibility he might hurt himself, or if he's throwing the tantrum in a busy place like a store, you can pick him up, hold him firmly and carry him to a quiet place. If the child is out of control, wrap your arms gently but firmly around him and hold him until he is calm. When holding a child in this manner, you do not cuddle him; your arms form a protective circle, and you are helping him control himself. While you are holding the child, you can encourage him to talk in a quiet voice and to express his real feelings calmly. You might say — striving to keep your own voice calm — "You're angry right now because you can't have that toy," or, "You're very disappointed because you don't want to leave the party." It is essential that you do not give in to the child's demands either during or immediately after the tantrum. If you suspect the child has a legitimate need you can say, "I can't understand until you tell me quietly," or, "Tell me calmly, then I'll try to help." Once the child has become calm and you discover he does need something, you can fulfill the need. Say something like, "Now that you've settled down I can see what's wrong and I can fix it."

Children learn to act spoiled when they know that their demands, screams, or tantrums will get them what they want. Parents often fall into a trap when their child first throws a tantrum — they give in immediately just to quiet him down. After the first experience, they make up their minds that they will not give in again. However, when the child throws another tantrum, the parents hold out for a few minutes longer than the first time, then they weaken and give in. As the child continues to throw tantrums, the parents often become increasingly inconsistent, sometimes giving in after a few minutes, sometimes longer, and sometimes not giving in at all. As this pattern continues, the child is learning to scream, yell, and kick for longer and longer periods of time. He knows, from experience, that someone will eventually give him what he wants. The adult who waits longer each time before giving in is helping the child develop the stamina he needs to throw increasingly lengthy tantrums. Once the child discovers the maximum amount of time he has to scream to get his own way, he is prepared to scream for that long, or for a little bit longer if necessary, to get what he wants. The key here is that the child is getting what he wants. In the best tradition of positive reinforcement, he is being *rewarded* for throwing longer and longer tantrums.

In many cases, the child is setting up the kind of testing situation we discussed in Chapter Two. He may be pushing his parents more to find out how far he can go than to obtain the simple momentary pleasure he is screaming for.

Tantrum throwing, when it is rewarded, is a type of behavior that spills over into other areas of life. As the child gets older he becomes demanding, self-centered, and bossy, and he tends to become furious when he doesn't get his own way.

The adults in a child's life contribute to the development of the self-centered personality not only by handling tantrums inconsistently, but also by being inconsistent in giving the child affection. Children need to be loved and wanted. If the parent does not have a sincere affection for the child or is so caught up in her own difficulties that she does not consistently show the affection she feels, the child may become very insecure. Often a child in this situation is treated as a precious darling one day and as if he doesn't exist the next. Because there is no logical connection between his behavior and how he is treated, the world becomes an uncertain place. In order to make his world seem more secure, and to feel that he can obtain the love he needs, he begins to manipulate people. Such children mistakenly feel that if they can control someone's behavior, they can also control their love.

Love and gifts don't spoil a child

Many people think that too much affection or too many material possessions spoil a child. Dr. Kason and I believe that lavish affection or excessive gifts spoil children when they are insincerely or inconsistently given. Real love is a positive force, and can have no ill effects. We believe that material gifts that are given in the spirit of true love are harmless.

Frequently, however, material gifts are not given in the spirit of love — especially when they are given in excess. If we look closely at why parents give excessively, we may discover the reason the gifts contribute to their children being spoiled. Parents and other adults are usually able to give any number of excuses for their out-of-balance giving. They often say they want to give their children everything they didn't get themselves; they say they want the child to know he is really, truly loved; sometimes they say they hope to make up to a child for what they felt he lost through divorce, the death of a parent, or being adopted. Many times the parents who have these feelings are well-meaning. But the fact remains that they feel inadequate about the love they have been giving to the child. Otherwise, they would not feel they had to embellish their affection with gifts.

In general, the reason parents give excessively is to cover up a subconscious fear that they do not really love their children enough or to rectify mistakes they feel they have made in the child's upbringing. Ironically, many times such people have been fairly good parents, and it is only their feelings of inadequacy that cause them to act this way. In some cases, however, the parents do not want the child or are not capable of loving him because of their own emotional inadequacies. These parents' excessive giving is frequently an attempt to cover up their feelings. These people may need to seek professional help. Often they were mistreated or inadequately cared for when they were children.

Other parents are terribly afraid they are not spending enough time with their children. In today's frantic world, this may indeed be the case. Of course, only the parents themselves can determine this. And, even if it is true, giving excessive gifts will not solve the problem.

Insincerity confuses kids

If a parent gives too many material possessions to cover up feelings of inadequacy, failure, or lack of love, she is not doing it out of a sincere or joyous desire to share. Children are intuitive, and they invariably sense the mixed emotions that prompted the gifts even if they are not consciously aware of it. Because there is a contradiction between why the adult says she is giving the gifts and why she is really doing it, the child feels insecure. As these feelings of uncertainty become more pronounced, the child may act out his confusion by misbehaving, or he might test the limits that have been set for him with demanding, spoiled behavior. Although he may seem to be crying out for more toys or for specific material objects, he may really be crying for sincere affection and an environment he can trust.

If this were not so, how could there be some children who have been given countless material possessions and yet who are not spoiled? I had the pleasure of watching two such boys as they grew up. They were given every material thing they could desire by their very wealthy parents. Family friends often voiced their opinion that the boys would be terribly spoiled by the gifts. The boys were, however, also encouraged to work and take responsibility for their actions. Their home life was not perfect, but the parents felt a sincere affection for the children and spent a good deal of time with them in family activities. They have both turned into hard-working adults, with generous natures, many friends, and well-adjusted families.

Children need love and touch

We have all heard people say, "Don't pick up the baby too much, it will spoil him." "Let him cry, he has to find out what life is like." "That child is going to be so spoiled, her mother picks her up all the time." These expressions are so common that most young parents are concerned about holding their baby too much. And yet North Americans live in one of the most touch-starved societies in the world. Scientists have shown that adequate physical touch is as important to sustaining an infant's life as food and shelter. Some people feel that by depriving a child of touch, cuddling, and kindness, they will help him grow into a "tough" adult. Ironically, it will. They will also teach him that the world is a lonely place and that other people cannot be counted on to give him the love and affection he needs.

Obviously, a parent cannot run to a baby every time he cries or give in to his every whim and desire. Parents are busy, and sometimes children must learn to wait. Parents also need to deal out appropriate consequences when they are necessary and feel confident when they ignore a child's tantrums. We believe, however, that it is wrong to intentionally leave a baby crying or to neglect his need for attention and physical affection because you are afraid it will spoil him.

Respond to a baby's needs

When it comes to the crunch — the baby is crying and the mother and father don't know whether they should pick him up — the parents have to decide what is best. Many experts feel a newborn should be attended to each time he cries, and that it is better to pick up and attend to a newborn too much than not enough. As the baby grows older, the parent can take a cue from the sound of his cries. Studies have proven something that many parents have always known: the sounds of a baby's crying actually differ depending on what he is trying to communicate. Attentive parents can learn to differentiate the cries. They can tell when their baby is crying because he is hungry, or fussing because he is wet, or screaming because he is in pain. They also know when he is crying because he needs to be held, loved or reassured that they are near.

Some parents who are aware of these differences still have difficulty making use of the information. Common sense would tell us that when a baby is crying because he is wet or hungry, or uncomfortable, we should remedy the situation as quickly as possible. When we are absolutely certain, on the other hand, that all the baby's needs have been met, and yet he persists in making half-hearted, whiney noises — probably to complain about feeling cranky — common sense also tells us this is an appropriate time to hold back, to wait and see if he will fall asleep or begin to entertain himself after a few minutes. When parents are unable to determine whether they should pick the baby up, we generally recommend that they go ahead and do it. We think it is far better to err on the side of giving a child too much attention than not giving him enough.

The key factor in all this is the question of whether the baby's needs have been met. Most parents have little trouble realizing that when a baby is hungry he needs to be fed or that when his diaper is wet he *needs* to be changed. But a baby also *needs* to be held, touched, and cuddled. Parents must be just as sure that their baby's need for attention is being met as they are that any other basic physical need is being taken care of. Keep this in mind when you hear someone say, "Oh, let the baby cry, he only wants someone to pick him up." It may be true that that is all the child wants, but it is also true that he may *need* to be picked up. He may need to know that you are close by and that you love him.

This doesn't mean that every single time the baby cries a little you have to drop what you're doing and run to him. This, especially when there are other young children in a home whose needs must be met, is simply not realistic. But it does mean that you, as a parent, have to recognize your baby's needs for attention and affection as being just as legitimate as any other need. It also means that you need to be attentive to what he is trying to communicate with his crying and respond accordingly. You can also be flexible. For instance, when the baby is crying to be picked up and you want him to go to sleep, you can try going to him and rubbing his tummy for a while without picking him up or you can simply stand in the door and speak to him in a warm, reassuring

Love, Limits and Consequences

voice. Every parent knows, of course, that there's always a chance the baby will break into a real howl as soon as he realizes that someone has entered the room. Still it's an alternative that often works and is worth the risk, since you'll be certain in your own mind that you've given the baby some reassurance.

The question of whether to pick the baby up is one of the most ticklish issues in parenting. No book, no authority can tell you how much to hold your child or when to pick him up. However, as long as you realize that your child's need for love, touch, and the warmth of physical contact is just as real as any other, you will have at least one good guideline to base your actions on. And remember that no child was ever spoiled by love.

What does — and does not — spoil a child

- ❑ Children need to grow in an atmosphere of love and affection — they're not spoiled by love.
- ❑ Getting inconsistent attention can cause a child to act spoiled.
- ❑ Giving in to or positively reinforcing negative behavior — like tantrums — causes kids to act spoiled.
- ❑ Feeling insecure, unloved and unwanted can cause a child to act spoiled. In this case excessive gifts make the matter worse.
- ❑ Demonstrate your love:
    - ▎ Say "I love you."
    - ▎ Give kids lots of hugs and kisses.
    - ▎ Give each child individual attention.
    - ▎ Sometimes your kids need time with you, and nothing else will do.

Guideline

Children need sincere, unconditional love and affection — spoiled children are the result of perceived lack of love, inconsistent discipline, and the rewarding of negative behavior.

Chapter Eight

Possessiveness is not love

A possessive parent stifles a child's self-confidence, makes her dependent on others, builds in her fears that may last a lifetime — and almost never realizes that he's doing it. If a parent never lets his child out of his sight, if he always insists on knowing what the child is doing, if he worries incessantly about her safety, if he lets the slightest sniffle keep her home from school, he is probably being far more protective than is good for his child.

I have worked with a number of troubled children, who have had extremely protective parents. These children's difficulties ranged from specific fears to severe emotional problems. Even though the overprotectiveness of the parent was not the only factor involved in these conditions, it was, in some cases, significant.

The words *possessive* and *over-protective* are often used interchangeably, although they do not mean the same thing. Overprotectiveness is a way of acting that often arises out of a parent's tendency to be possessive. The result can be a smothering atmosphere. I saw an example of overprotectiveness the first time I worked with children. I was in high school and had a summer job teaching five-year-olds to swim.

Too much concern for safety

One of my students was a girl named Sheila. Her mother drove her nearly forty miles to our municipal swimming pool. When the other mothers dropped off their children and went for coffee, Sheila's mother lingered. Our wise director had banned parents from the premises during swimming instruction, but Sheila's mother stood outside the fence around the pool. In those days I had never heard of body language, and I was unaware that our stance and appearance can tell a lot about us. Still Sheila's mother's appearance made an impact on me. She would stand with her hands on the chain-link fence. Her knuckles were white with the force of her grasp. She wore a coat, which made no impression on me at the time, but today I realize it was significant. The air might have had a bit of a chill on a June morning, but no one needed a coat. The mother's dress showed that she was fearful of taking a chill on a summer day. Her face and hands showed that she was terrified about her daughter's safety.

If she was making an impact on me, imagine the effect she was having on Sheila. It took me more than a week to get Sheila to put more than her feet in the water. Once I had gently coaxed her into the water, she clutched my neck so tightly she made marks on my skin. When I tried to venture a few feet from the edge with her, she began to scream and cry pathetically. Finally, the pool director ordered the mother to stay away. Within a week Sheila was splashing joyfully in the water with the other children.

I wonder if some of the phobias we believe have been caused by traumatic experiences such as near drowning have not instead been caused by fears parents unknowingly instill in their children.

Coddled kids aren't well-liked

A parent's protectiveness can affect a child's behavior to the point that he is not accepted by his peers. In one special school for problem children, I worked with a twelve-year-old boy named Tim who had a very overprotective mother. Tim's mother fussed so much over how he was dressed, what he ate, and what he did that Tim, too, developed this fretful attitude. At lunchtime Tim picked over his food like an old fussbudget. He was extremely conscious of his health and would not go outside for a moment without his hat, mittens, and boots. Even when the winter broke into spring, Tim was afraid it wasn't quite warm enough for him to go without his mittens. Never missing a chance to tease him, the other boys would hide his hat and mittens in the school. Tim would cry and throw tantrums until the mittens were returned. Tim was also set apart from the other children by his mother's fear of allowing him to take the bus to or from school. Tim was the only child who was driven to school and picked up afterward. All these factors combined to make Tim an outcast in the school, and the object of the other children's ridicule — all because he had never been allowed to do anything on his own. Consequently, he did not have any of the spunk and daring that makes a twelve-year-old boy adventurous and likable.

Overprotectiveness can hold kids back

Many educators and psychologists think a parent's extreme overprotectiveness can keep a child from maturing or developing properly. This process is known as infantilization. The parent, often the mother, does everything for the child to the degree that the child does not learn to do anything for herself. For example, the parents might continue to feed and dress a child for years longer than necessary. It is possible for such a condition to actually disrupt the child's natural maturation processes and cause her to be functionally retarded or to have severe emotional problems. Alisa was such a child. When she was sixteen years old, she had the maturity of a six- or eight-year-old child. When Alisa's mother visited the clinic she would button Alisa's coat for her, tie her shoes, put her mittens on her, and scold her as if she were a toddler.

Alisa would coo like a baby when her mother looked after her. The mother seemed totally unaware that Alisa was able to perform these tasks on her own, and, in fact, had to when her mother wasn't there. The professionals at the clinic were wise to Alisa. They knew she had many abilities, and they treated her as a young adult. Their treatment of Alisa had a tremendous positive effect, but it did not solve her problem. After four months at the clinic Alisa stopped acting like a baby. By her second year there her academic performance had gone from a grade-three to a grade-six level. These improvements were evident, however, only when her mother wasn't around.

Eventually we insisted that Alisa be taken to a psychologist for further testing. We were convinced that she was not mentally retarded and that her problems were emotional. After a few visits the psychologist summed up the tragedy of her situation. He told us he could not help Alisa make long-term improvements as long as she remained with her mother. He said, "The problem is not Alisa's, it is her mother's."

Give kids room to grow

The examples of Alisa and Tim may seem a little extreme — and they are. However, both children came from apparently average families and both had well-adjusted brothers and sisters; their stories give us good examples of just how detrimental a factor overprotectiveness can be in the relationship between certain parents and certain children. Stories like Sheila's are more common, and help us realize that every parent needs to give every child the room she needs to learn about life for herself.

It is a characteristic of overprotective parents to hover around their child each time she attempts something new and to rush to her aid the moment she begins to falter. This attitude does a great disservice to the child. The saying "we learn by making mistakes" has become a platitude, but it is still true. A child learns to master a task by attempting it again and again. Take the example of a child who is playing with a toy that has holes of different shapes and wooden blocks that fit through the holes. The adult who feels compelled to put the piece of wood through the hole for the child as soon as she has a bit of difficulty is not helping the child. He is cheating her out of a chance to learn. A better and less protective approach is for the adult to first make sure the toy is appropriate for the child's age, show her how to work it, then let her be. If the child shows signs of becoming unduly frustrated, the adult can step in and help the child accomplish the task for herself, for instance, by handing her a piece and pointing to the right hole, or by taking her hand and helping her position the piece so it slides easily through the hole. If the child isn't becoming too frustrated, it's better to let her play: if she can't master the task she will probably come up with a more creative way to play with the toy.

Where to draw the line

No parent wants to be overprotective or possessive; he wants to protect his child from harm and to love her. But love cannot flourish in a stifling atmosphere. A parent who sincerely wants to avoid possessiveness must draw the line between being over-protective and being safety-conscious. The key for most parents is probably simple, honest self-evaluation. The possessive parent tends to be the one who has little confidence in himself and tries to compensate for what he fears are his shortcomings by over-doing his job as a parent. This parent tends to worry about everything in his life. He is especially afraid that something will happen to his children because of some fault of his own. He feels that watching over them with an eagle eye will prevent anything from harming them. He may, when his children reach adolescence, become excessively strict; for instance, he may set unreasonable curfews or refuse to let his children participate in normal activities. The possessive parent often subconsciously fears he does not care about his children enough — and his overprotectiveness is a type of overcompensation. Or he may be someone who was wild when he was young and who is terrified his children will get into the same kind of trouble he did.

I know of no set rules for determining what constitutes possessiveness or overprotectiveness in parents. Being aware that such a tendency exists and that it can have a profoundly negative effect on a child helps most parents curb their possessiveness. However, if a parent becomes aware that he is being overprotective and finds he cannot help himself, he should seek professional help in overcoming his difficulty.

Even though safety is one of the most important factors to consider in a child's upbringing, children can be given a great deal of freedom in a safe environment. This helps them develop independence and self-confidence. In our society we tend to think a lot more about taking care of and protecting our children than we do about letting them go. Yet both processes need to be going on as we raise our children. It is important for parents to learn to let go of the strings gradually and gracefully from the time the independent two-year-old strikes out on her own to the time the young adult moves away from home. When parents give their children more independence as time goes on, they are able to accept the children's independence and adulthood without any lasting sense of loss or unhappiness.

The same thing is true for teachers and other adults who work closely with children. I know I have had to battle against being too protective of the children I work with. Teachers and day-care workers need to remember that the eight or twelve hours a day they spend with the children are tremendously influential, and that smothering a child with concern during these hours does nothing to help her develop.

Many children of well-meaning but overprotective parents grow up to lead well-balanced lives and succeed in school and society. Yet a major upheaval often occurs when the young adult decides to move into her own apartment, to marry a person different from the family standard, or to choose a profession other than the one desired by the parents. Many children grow up and do some of these things, but in the possessive parents' eyes, the child's natural evolutionary wish to be independent and find her own heart's desire represents rejection and lack of love. Ironically, the child who does become independent is the only one who is free enough to really love her parents.

Possessiveness is not love

Avoid overprotectiveness

- ❏ Keep concerns for health and safety reasonable.
- ❏ Allow kids room to grow.
- ❏ Allow kids room to try things for themselves and make their own mistakes.
- ❏ Remember overprotectiveness can hold kids back.

Guideline

Children need the freedom to grow and make mistakes — within reasonable limits.

Chapter Nine

I'll never do that when I grow up

Almost every child at one time or another vows he will never treat his own children the way he is being treated. I remember promising myself as a child that I would never scold my children for spilling their milk. I am sure most of us remember yelling something like, "Boy, I'll *never* hit my kids when I grow up!"

In spite of our glowing promises, if we carefully examine our relationships with children once we reach adulthood, we will be shocked to find that we treat our children much the same way our parents treated us. We find ourselves exploding over a glass of spilled milk or lashing out in anger with the same physical abuse we received as children. As the human race evolves, it is natural that each generation finds improved ways of raising children. Yet we often find ourselves unable to apply these new and better ways; we find ourselves reverting to the mistakes we swore we would never make.

Many psychologists have come to the conclusion that we tend to raise our children the way we were raised. In *Born to Win*, Muriel James and Dorothy Jongeward say: "In many cases people automatically tend to rear their children as they were reared." They cite the example of a man who vowed he would never beat his children the way his father beat him. However, when he had a son of his own he found it "natural" to beat him. The man was confused and ashamed. He felt his behavior was wrong, but he didn't know how to correct it.

Many parents and teachers share this man's frustration. One young woman, who had been brought up by a nagging mother, said, "You know, I sound just like my own mother when I nag my kids. My *voice* even sounds the same. I can't stand it, but I can't seem to stop." In my home, my father was fussy about table manners. The table was always beautifully set, and dinner was a formal affair. If I didn't eat a particular food properly my father would lecture me unpleasantly. If I spilled something or accidentally made a mess he would suddenly become angry. During my training in education and psychology, I learned that there were important emotional components to eating and that mealtime should be a warm, comfortable affair. I learned that food is associated with love in a child's mind and that, for young children, playing with food is an important sensory experience. I came to *believe* these things; I *knew* that they were true; but when I first started working in a clinical setting where young children were allowed to mess with their food, it took every bit of willpower I possessed to keep from interfering. When a child spilled his milk, I had to bite my tongue to keep from shouting the way my father would have.

Unfortunately, some people confuse common sense with the destructive patterns of behavior they absorbed in childhood. They may think it is common sense to lock their children in a closet for punishment; they may think they are justified in beating a child because it will save him from going to hell later on; they may think it makes sense to let a child touch the stove so he will know not to do it again. What these people think of as common sense is really the voices of their misguided parents and teachers coming back to them.

Why we discipline like our parents did

Fortunately, the tendency to repeat patterns we experienced in childhood can be overcome. But first we must understand why the pattern occurs. We need to look at certain discoveries about the mind made about thirty years ago by a neurosurgeon named Wilder Penfield.

Dr. Penfield did a series of experiments in which he used electrodes to stimulate a part of the brain called the temporal cortex. He discovered that when particular spots on the cortex were stimulated, the person whose brain was being stimulated would automatically recollect, in great detail, certain events from his past that were long forgotten. The stimulation of different points on the cortex would produce different recollections. Many of these recollections were of insignificant events, and Dr. Penfield eventually came to the conclusion that all our past experiences — not just important ones — were stored in the brain.

There were several significant points about Dr. Penfield's discoveries. First, the recollection was *involuntary*. In other words, the subject could not stop himself from remembering the event once his cortex had been stimulated. Second, the subject would *relive* or *reexperience* the event. He could neither stop nor control the flood of memories even though he knew they were being artificially stimulated. Third, Dr. Penfield discovered that a person could reexperience the emotions he had felt during a long-forgotten event even if he didn't consciously remember the event itself.

Many stimuli — not just electrodes — can cause the subconscious mind to replay experiences from our past. Often we reexperience emotions without having a conscious awareness of where the feelings are coming from. For example, for years, every time I heard a certain song, I felt a flood of sorrow washing over me, and felt unloved and rejected. I was aware the song depressed me, but I had no idea why. One day I tried an exercise that helped me consciously remember the event I subconsciously associated with the song. I remembered that, when I was about fifteen, a boy I believed I was in love with told me he wanted to break up. While he was telling me this, we were sitting in his car in front of my house and the song was playing on the car radio.

Programming from childhood

Psychologists and doctors have used Dr. Penfield's discoveries to help them understand certain tendencies parents have when raising children. In *I'm Okay, You're Okay*, Dr. Thomas Harris states that the mind has recorded "all the admonitions and rules and laws that the child heard from his parents and saw in their living. They range all the way from the earliest parental communications, interpreted nonverbally through tone of voice, facial expression, cuddling, or non-cuddling, to the more elaborate verbal rules and regulations espoused by the parents as the little person became able to understand words." According to Harris these rules, right or wrong, are recorded in the child's brain as "truth." In a sense, the child's brain is programmed much the way a computer is.

When children grow up and are parents, their children's actions sometimes trigger the subconscious mind, and memories of similar situations are replayed. Parents find themselves suddenly using the words their parents used and reacting the way their parents did. Because these responses are based on childhood programming, they are automatic and involuntary. Often parents find themselves doing something they swore they would never do and are terribly disappointed in themselves.

Changing old programming

Parents can change their programming. First, they must learn to recognize when programming is causing a certain reaction. Certain clues can help. One clue is the use of expressions that were heard repeatedly when the adult was a child. For example: "If I've told you once, I've told you a thousand times," "If you do that once more I'll..." When an adult hears herself using these expressions, she can be fairly sure she is acting from subconscious prodding rather than logic. Of course, the expressions each adult heard again and again in emotionally loaded situations as a child were different. Thus, each adult must discover which expressions have meaning for her. The expressions themselves aren't necessarily important; they are simply a clue that memories may be causing an adult to act in a way she may not want to act. Once she discovers old programming she wants to change, the adult must make a definite, concentrated effort to do so.

Often the key to success lies in finding a new, positive habit to replace the old, negative one, or in learning different methods for handling particular problems. The parent, for instance, who was slapped as a child and finds she has a tendency to want to slap her own children can teach herself to replace hitting with a reasonable consequence, like sending the child for a time out. First, the parent must make a conscious and concerted effort to stop the unwanted behavior. Then she must practice substituting a new behavior for the old one until the new behavior becomes automatic.

Love, Limits and Consequences

I have seen parents make heroic efforts to replace old programs, which were harmful to their children, with new, positive parenting skills. One parent was the daughter of two alcoholics. She had been neglected and rejected as a child and had received almost no physical affection or warm contact from her parents. She grew up, was well-educated, and became a successful professional woman. But when she married and became pregnant, she was terrified. In desperation, she considered abortion. She didn't know where her deep-rooted fear of having a child came from. Finally she realized she was afraid she would reject and refuse to touch her child, just as her parents had done. Once she became aware of the pattern, she felt fairly certain she could change it. Her fears about having a child diminished. When her son was born, she still experienced many difficulties. She found it especially hard to touch him or give him physical affection. Then she would remind herself that she didn't want to hold or caress her baby only because she had rarely been held or caressed herself. As part of her determined effort to change her old programming and become a physically affectionate mother, she had to make a schedule of times when she would play with and hold the baby. In the beginning she had to force herself to keep the schedule. She even created a behavioral reward chart in her mind: to "earn" a cup of coffee, she had to spend a certain amount of time cuddling the baby. As the days went by, she played with him for longer and longer periods of time. After a while she found herself enjoying it. She no longer needed to remind herself to give the baby attention; it came naturally. About the time the boy turned six, I was speaking with his mother. I saw her face glow with love as she spoke of his success in school and his ability to get along with others. This parent was able to change because of her understanding of herself and because of her determination.

Although many people don't have such serious problems, most of us have at least a few patterns we would like to change. I knew one teacher whose parents had been overprotective perfectionists. Once she made an effort to become aware of how old patterns were affecting her teaching, she realized that she was far too demanding of the children, asking for neatness and perfection their small hands could not master. She also discovered she was too concerned about safety and often intervened in harmless games at recess. As she worked on these problems, she became more tolerant of the children's mistakes and more confident and trusting of their abilities. She found her rapport and success with her students increased along with her effort to correct her overprotective and demanding ways.

Some parents and teachers tend to reject the way they were raised so completely that they swing to the other side of the spectrum: if their parents were overly strict with them, they become extremely permissive; if their parents disciplined them too harshly, they never discipline their children. This overreaction to upbringing can also be harmful to our children. Again, the key is to change old programming. First we have to become aware of what we are doing; then we must make a conscious decision to change; finally, we need to replace the negative patterns with positive ones.

When to go for professional help

Some people require professional help in overcoming their programming, for example people who batter or sexually abuse a child, and people who neglect a child's needs. Statistics show that most of these people were themselves battered, molested, or neglected, and that the horrible habit is passed down from generation to generation. The effects of child abuse are so deep and ingrained it may be impossible to overcome them without professional help. Anyone who has suffered abuse or neglect as a child will probably need to seek out such help. And everyone should feel comfortable about asking for assistance if they feel they need it. Doctors, therapists, ministers, and parent groups are all there to help. Many large cities also have anonymous phone-in lines that parents can call when they feel "the kids are driving them crazy."

Over the years, Dr. Kason and I have worked with children who have been battered, neglected, abused, ridiculed, and emotionally mistreated by their parents. We have seen children who have been humiliated, discouraged, and convinced they were stupid by teachers. But we never met a parent or teacher who started out with the *intention* of doing a bad job. They either did not know any better, or they were not able to control the psychological pressures that caused them to act in destructive ways.

Dr. Kason and I are convinced that most parents, teachers, and child-care workers want to do the best they can for the young lives they touch. We all need to spend some time thinking about the ways in which we were raised and taught. We need to sift carefully through our backgrounds and decide where we can improve. We must watch carefully for the times when the old habits we are unhappy with slip into our interactions with children. Remember that there never was a perfect parent, that each one of us will make mistakes as all parents before us have done. But if we can treat our children with love, respect, and unconditional warm regard, the mistakes will not matter.

Learning new parenting habits

- ❏ Most parents tend to treat their children the way they were treated when they were young.
- ❏ The discipline methods our parents — and sometimes our teachers — used on us are programmed into our subconscious minds.
- ❏ This programming tends to spring into action whenever we are involved in discipline situations with our kids.
- ❏ If we think the discipline methods our parents used need to be improved, we have to make a big effort to learn new and more appropriate ones.
- ❏ We can then use these methods to replace the old ones. This often takes a strong effort.
- ❏ People who were abused as children often need to get professional help to change their programming.

Guideline

We tend — without realizing it — to treat our children the way we were treated. We have to make a real effort to learn new and appropriate methods to replace inappropriate ones.

Chapter Ten

Troubleshooting

Many of the difficulties that arise in the daily lives of children could be prevented if adults would learn to be effective troubleshooters. Although the term troubleshooter is relatively modern, it brings to my mind the image of a hero of the old west. I always think of the man who rode "shotgun" on the old stagecoaches. He sat next to the driver, diligently surveying the countryside and approaching riders. To be good at his job he had to be a keen judge of character, and he had to have a powerful sixth sense. He knew when something was about to go wrong, and was able to prevent it. Although far from being shining heroes, adults don't really have much difficulty filling the boots of this kind of a troubleshooter in their dealings with children. In fact, we are convinced that as adults, it is one of our most important functions.

Children are emotionally charged. Their lives are filled with ups and downs, conflicts, jealousies, joys, passions, and uncertainties. Invariably certain times and certain situations that lead to trouble. Children are so busy with the important job of experiencing that they almost never think ahead. Adults need to develop an eye for situations that are likely to lead to trouble and learn to be prepared for the times of day that are most difficult for children to handle. When a parent or teacher sees trouble brewing, he can step in and prevent the problem.

In-between times

Bruno Bettelheim, a renowned psychologist who worked for many years with emotionally disturbed children, discovered there were certain periods during the day that were difficult for these children to handle. He called them "in-between times." These times are, frequently, the interludes that occur between the end of one activity and the beginning of the next. Stable children have less difficulty with these periods than disturbed children do, but in-between times are something an effective troubleshooter needs to be aware of. Some in-between times occur at waking, at bedtime, and when a child is leaving the house for school — or any time an activity ends, for instance, when a young child has to interrupt her playing to eat or take a bath.

When a day is flowing as usual, in-between times don't cause much trouble. However, anytime there is extra anticipation or dread in the air, the adult needs to be on his toes. Waking up, for instance, doesn't mean just getting up, it means going to school, and if a child happens to be worried about a homework project or an activity that has been planned for the day, her concern can manifest itself in anger at being awakened, morning grumpiness or arguments over which clothes she is going to wear. If a child is having a bad time at school for any reason — poor grades, inability to make friends, an unkind teacher — the period between waking up and getting out the door may be fraught with tears or sudden, unexplained illnesses. It is also a time when fights will tend to break out between a child who is doing poorly in school and a brother or sister who is doing well.

Too much anticipation

Leaving the house to go anywhere the child sees as unpleasant is a potentially difficult time. However, leaving for an anticipated event can often pose just as much of a problem. Many parents have wondered what would cause their child to blow up before a long-awaited event; they can't understand why she isn't thrilled and happy. The explanation is that when a child has been waiting for something, like a trip to the zoo, for a long time, she has a great deal at stake. She may be afraid that something could go wrong and prevent the trip. She might be concerned that the outing won't live up to her expectations. Or she might not know how to handle her overflowing excitement. She is not consciously aware of these factors, but they affect her mood. Sometimes a very small incident will throw her off balance. In the case of an insecure child or one who is going through a difficult time — for example, a family breakup — the reaction can be so severe that the trip must be called off. This is sometimes a relief to a troubled child because she no longer has to deal with the conflicting emotions she feels.

There might also be some detail about the trip that the child is uncomfortable with or uncertain about. A friend of mine who was recently divorced was planning to take her son to her annual company picnic. It was an outing her son had always enjoyed, and she couldn't understand why she was having so much difficulty with him when they were getting ready to go. He argued about what shoes he was going to wear, he whined about the food she was packing — items that were usually his favorites — and finally he threw a fit when he wasn't allowed to take along a certain toy. Later, she realized her son had felt uncertain about the trip because she planned to meet a man she had recently started dating at the picnic. She had casually mentioned the fact to her son and hadn't thought much about it because her son had already met the man and seemed to like him. She had not stopped to consider, however, how it might effect her son to see this gentleman at a function his father had always attended in the past. The mother realized she could have prevented the difficulties if she had taken the time to talk to her son and help him understand that he might be feeling a little sad because the picnic was something they had always done as a family. She could have reassured him that the man they were meeting was not trying to replace his father, but was just meeting them there to have a good time.

Bedtime and other in-between times

Probably the most difficult in-between time for any child is bedtime. It is a time when an enjoyable activity has to end, and it is a nebulous time that hangs somewhere between light and dark, waking and sleeping, fellowship and aloneness. Night may mean many things to a child that an adult is not aware of. The child may be having frightening dreams that she doesn't talk to anyone about, she may be afraid of the dark and ashamed to tell anyone, or she may have seen a frightening movie that troubles her subconsciously. If a child has few friends, night can seem like a time of exaggerated aloneness. It might also represent the imminence of another rough day at school. The more secure and happy a child is, the easier bedtime will be for her. But *all* children go through difficult periods and times of feeling insecure.

Any major change in routine is, in a certain sense, an in-between time and can create problems. Moving to a new house, taking a trip, or even changing bedrooms can make a child feel unsettled and insecure. At these times parents need to be aware of their children's feelings, and need to be especially reassuring. Parents must take the time to explain the changes in routine to the children in advance and to give them an outline of exactly what is going to happen, and when.

Mealtime

Adults need to be extremely sensitive at mealtimes, too. It is important for parents to think about the feelings that surround the giving of food. It has often been said that food represents love. It is the first thing a baby gets from her parents. The baby is held and snuggled as she drinks from the breast or bottle. Thus, a connection is developed in a child's mind between eating and love, and we believe this connection never disappears. Food means more to children than something to eat, and mealtime can be an emotionally charged time.

This is especially true if a child was fed roughly as a baby or if she has unhappy memories associated with mealtimes. Several years ago I was visiting someone for dinner. At the table the woman of the house screamed at her noisy children, "Why do you kids always fight at the table? We have company!" I knew the answer well from many previous visits: the parents always fought at the table. These weren't little spats or quarrels, but serious and sometimes violent arguments.

I became aware of how strongly children feel about food while I was working in a school for troubled children. The school was in a large Victorian house with a cozy kitchen. The children were allowed to help themselves to the school food supply. Almost all the children came from embittered homes, which were either broken or in constant conflict. Every day at lunchtime all but two of the children would ceremoniously throw away the lunches that had been prepared for them at home and eat the food provided by the school. This food was often prepared by the children; sometimes it consisted of exotic or experimental dishes prepared by the staff. No matter how tasteless or unusual the school food was, the children always preferred it. The food prepared at home represented the scolding, criticism, and mistrust they received at home. Because everything they received at home was negative, they felt subconsciously that the food they received contained these negative feelings.

If a parent suddenly realizes his child might have such feelings about food, or if mealtime has become an unhappy time in a household, he will probably want to change the situation immediately. It is only fair to say that children who have problems with meals may be covering up a great deal of hostility, and sometimes professional help is called for. Generally, however, most problems surrounding mealtime can be prevented by effective troubleshooting. The parent, teacher, or child-care worker needs to remember that meals are rough for any child who is going through a difficult period. Adults need to be aware that food represents more to a child than something to eat. Food should be served in a loving manner. Arguments and criticism should be banned from the table. Of course, none of these techniques will work if the children aren't allowed to express their anger and feelings in the ways we discuss in Chapter Eleven.

Group play

Troubleshooting can be valuable any time a group or a couple of children are playing together. Certain times are bound to bring on a battle, and the adult who wants to prevent trouble needs to be on the lookout for them. They include: a new toy that only one child can play with at a time; a popular game that only a few children can play; and group games in which two children have to choose teams. In fact, almost any seemingly innocuous childhood game in which one child calls on another can breed trouble, as the popular children tend to get picked first and the less popular often get left out. Any game in which the loser is singled out can cause trouble.

Certain ways children act can also serve as warning signs. Excessive bragging — not just talking or boasting a little about an accomplishment — is a sign that a particular child is feeling pretty bad about herself, and the bragging usually irritates the other children. Trouble is also usually afoot when one child starts complaining about something not being fair, or when one starts to grab at a toy another is playing with. The adult needs to be on his toes any time there is a switch in allegiance within a group of children. This can be a particular problem when three children are playing together, since one is always left out if two suddenly become chummy.

It is also important to remember that children don't have the tolerance levels adults do. Even when parents and teachers are doing their best, situations sometimes arise in which the children become overtired, get too hot, or have to wait too long for their food. When this occurs the wise adult knows that trouble may break out and does his best to diffuse tension before it has a chance to build up.

How to troubleshoot

The first step in effective troubleshooting is to be aware of difficult situations. Then the adult should verbally clarify the situation as soon as he senses a problem. In this way the adult helps the child become aware of her feelings. As we explain in Chapter Eleven, the adult doesn't need to sit down and have a long, philosophical discussion with the child about her feelings. He can accomplish his purpose with a few simple, appropriately placed remarks. If, for example, the child becomes hyper the day before an outing, the adult can help her see why she feels this way by saying, "I see you're getting really excited about going to the zoo tomorrow. It's okay to be excited, but I think you'd better slow down a little." If the child is getting too upset about a small thing on the day of the outing, the parent or teacher might say something like, "I bet you're getting a little too excited about going to the zoo. Do you have any questions? Is there anything you're worried about?"

Dr. Kason and I use this technique all the time in our dealings with children. It helps them understand their feelings, and it provides a perfect opportunity for them to become aware of alternatives.

It is also a good idea to clarify the situation when problems with toys or games arise. One day at school, I was about to let five children have their recess period. One said, "I want to play Sorry." "So do I," chorused the other four. I could see there was going to be a problem, because only four children can play Sorry at a time. I said, "Hold it. It looks to me like we're about to have a hassle. Only four people can play this game, and someone's going to be left out and feel bad. I suggest you pick a game five can play or settle on two different games. I don't think anyone should be left out." The children agreed and came up with a solution: the youngest said she wouldn't mind playing another game. One of the older boys said he would play with her. The other three asked if they could still play Sorry. All the children had a peaceful recess.

When one child is playing with an attractive toy and it's clear another child wants it, the adult can clarify the situation by saying something like, "Billy, I can see you would really like to play with the truck Jenny has. But she just started playing with it, and you'll have to wait a little while." Later, if Billy still wants the truck, the adult can say, "Okay, why don't you ask Jenny nicely if she'll let you play with it now." If it is a communal toy that has to be shared, the adult might say, "Jenny, you'll need to share that truck in a little while. Why don't you play with it for ten more minutes, then give Billy a chance. I'll tell you when the time's about up." Setting a time limit is often a good trouble shooting technique.

Whenever a child wants something that isn't available a potential for trouble exists. One of the best ways to troubleshoot in this situation with young children is to encourage fantasy. If a child starts to cry because she wants a cookie — and there are no cookies available — the adult can say, "If I had a magic wand, I'd give you a whole truckload of cookies!" A child often responds by saying what *she* would do if she had a magic wand, and the trouble is avoided. Sometimes a child can be distracted from a temporary desire by a game of wishful thinking. If the child says, "I wish I had a cookie," the adult can say, "I wish I had a boatload of cookies!" The child might say, "Well, I wish I had an *ocean* of cookies." The game goes on, and trouble is once again prevented.

Another tool the troubleshooter can use is to let children know well in advance when anything out of the ordinary is going to happen. It's also necessary to go over the entire schedule with them. If, for instance, one of the kids has to see the doctor in the afternoon, the parent might say at breakfast, "Brent, I just want to remind you that today's the day we go to the doctor for your checkup. You'll have all morning to play outside, but right after lunch we'll get ready and go. We have to be there at two o'clock."

Adults need to remember that telling a child once about a change in routine is usually not enough. This is especially true for outings and very special events. When a trip to the zoo is planned, for instance, the parent or teacher might say, "On Saturday we're going to the zoo. We're leaving home at ten o'clock. It takes about an hour to get there. We'll eat lunch at the zoo, we'll see the animals, and we'll come home about four o'clock." The child should be reminded of the facts as often as needed, and all her questions about the trip — or any other change in routine — should be answered. Younger children will need to be reminded more often than older ones. Still, children of all ages are comforted by knowing in detail what's ahead and by having an opportunity to ask questions about things that might be bothering them.

Sometimes effective troubleshooting involves separating certain children temporarily or changing plans. Sometimes it calls for firm action. It might even necessitate getting professional help for a child who is having difficulty with bedtime, school, or relationships. More than any one specific thing, however, troubleshooting is an attitude an adult has when he's being attentive, intuitive, and caring. A troubleshooter is tuned in to what's happening with the children around him.

Of course, this shouldn't be overdone. No child appreciates an adult who is always poking his nose into children's affairs. But she *does* like it when someone helps her learn how to spot trouble before she gets into it.

Troubleshooting

How to troubleshoot

- ❏ Be aware that there are times of the day and situations when flare-ups are likely to occur.

- ❏ Be on the lookout for these situations. Be tuned in and sensitive during these times of the day.

- ❏ Clarify the situation for the kids. Say, for example, "Jessie, I can see you really want to play with that brand-new truck of Bernie's."

- ❏ Help them understand that there is potential for trouble. Say, "Unfortunately, I don't think he's going to let you play with it right now. He's only had it a little while and he doesn't seem ready to share it." Or say, "I can see we're going to have a fight on our hands, if you don't quit bugging him about it."

- ❏ Break up a negative situation by suggesting an alternative or by getting the child to suggest an alternative. Say, for example: "Since you're not going to be able to play with Bernie's truck, why don't you think about another toy you'd like to play with — tell me, then I'll help you find it."

- ❏ If the child's emotions have already gotten control of her, use active listening (see Chapter Eleven) to help her express herself and deal with her frustration. Then discuss alternative activities or more appropriate behavior.

Be ready to troubleshoot

- During in-between times.
- At meal times.
- At bedtime.
- During group play, especially when there are three or more children playing.
- During games where "captains" choose "teams."
- Before trips, outing, special events.
- During any upset in the normal routine.
- Anytime one child is feeling particularly disappointed or bad about herself.

Guideline

Think like a troubleshooter! Be aware of potential problems. Use your common sense and intuition to prevent hassles before they begin.

Chapter Eleven

It's all right to cry

There is little doubt that the happiest, most well-adjusted adults are those who have learned to express their emotions honestly, openly, and appropriately. In spite of this, very few children today are learning this important skill as part of their daily upbringing. A number of cultures teach children, especially males, that they must learn to hide their emotions, and the Anglo-Saxon cultures of today may someday be looked upon as being some of the most emotionally suppressed the world has known. Even though there has been a great deal of talk in North America in the past two decades about things like "expressing yourself" and "doing your own thing," the number of violent crimes committed by people with severely suppressed emotions is increasing. Psychologists, sociologists, and law-enforcement officers who work with criminals are aware that the most destructive and gruesome crimes are often committed by the quiet individual who never expressed himself. How often after a terrible crime has been committed have we heard a neighbor interviewed on the news say, "Who would have ever suspected? He was such a quiet boy..."

Although the suppression of emotions does not always lead to violent crime, there are numerous ways in which it affects an individual. One of these is in the tragic end of many marriages and relationships. According to studies done by Marcia Lasswell, the associate director of the University of Southern California's marriage and family counselling program, the suppression of emotions, particularly in men, is a frequent factor in marriage breakdown. Depression and a number of other neuroses in children, adolescents and adults are often related to the suppression of feelings, particularly anger.

Medical evidence shows that suppressed emotions can also play a part in diseases such as ulcers, heart attacks, and high blood pressure. Suppressed rage has been found to be a factor in some cases of asthma and allergies, and there may be a relationship between suppressed emotions and hysterical illness.

Even though it is generally accepted that a difficulty with emotional expression begins in childhood, little has been said about what can be done about it during childhood. Emphasis has been placed instead on helping adults who suppress emotions to express their feelings through therapy, group sessions, or counseling. Unfortunately, the only people who receive any help in this area while they are still children are those who exhibit such extreme emotional disturbance that they are placed in play therapy or counseling with a trained expert.

Expressing emotions is healthy

It is perhaps time parents and teachers begin to recognize the importance of helping children express their emotions appropriately. It is natural for children to express their emotions; they begin to suppress them only when they *learn* this behavior from adults and older children. When children cry, we tell them to stop. We say, "Real men don't cry," "Big girls don't cry," "Don't be a big baby." In doing this, many psychologists feel we actually teach people to suppress their emotions. Lasswell mentions this in her report and adds that when we learn "to suppress feelings of anxiety, fear or hurt [we] may put a damper on the expression of feelings such as joy and excitement."

Once a parent or teacher is aware of the importance of emotional expression she can help a child learn to express his emotions appropriately. The word *appropriately* is a key here. Dr. Kason and I have seen parents get so carried away with letting their children express themselves that the children became menaces. In one family I knew, the little girl bit people she did not like; one of the two small boys sawed up the living-room coffee table one day, and the other set fire to the garage. Although I am sure the parents did not condone these specific activities, they never helped the children understand the difference between *appropriate* and *inappropriate* emotional expression. The parent or teacher who wants to help a child express himself appropriately can do so by developing an accepting attitude about emotions in general.

Many years ago Carl Rogers, a widely respected psychologist, developed a type of therapy that helped people express and clarify their emotions. Virginia Axline and other psychologists applied Rogers' ideas to their work with children with amazing success. Rogers' basic ideas have been modified so that special-education teachers can use them to help children express themselves. Although the use of Rogers' theories in therapy requires extensive training, the basic ideas can be applied by anyone. These ideas help the adult develop a nonjudgmental and accepting attitude toward children's emotions. Rogers' technique is now being used by a number of different parenting schools. Dr. Fitzhugh Dodson, in his book *How to Discipline With Love,* for instance, calls it the "feedback" technique, Adlerians and the proponents of Parent-Effectiveness Training call it "active listening."

The use of any of these techniques involves the development of a very definite, *accepting* attitude about emotional expression. Although learning how to use the methods is a relatively simple process, it is not always easy to carry them out because few of us were raised to think that expressing our emotions is acceptable.

Listening, understanding, responding

Once you are comfortable with the idea that it is necessary for a child to find ways to express his emotions appropriately, you can begin to use a listening technique based on Rogers' ideas. Rogerians call this the empathic response. You feel empathy for someone when you are able to put yourself in his shoes and understand how he's feeling. The word *empathic* conveys the sense of warmth, understanding, and acceptance that is important for the adult to have with children. The word *response* reminds the person using the technique that the way she responds is of paramount importance.

There are three steps in the empathic response. First, the parent or teacher must listen when a child is expressing his emotions and neither argue with nor deny those emotions. Next, the adult takes a moment to understand exactly *what* the child is feeling and *why* he is feeling that way. Finally, the adult responds in a loving and supportive way that helps the child identify both the emotion and its causes. Then the adult waits for the child to speak again.

Here's an example: A mother walks into a room and sees her six-year-old, Sarah, grab a stuffed toy away from her four-year-old, Kevin. Kevin screams, "Mommy, I hate Sarah!" The mother sizes up the situation, then says, "Kevin, I can see you're really angry because Sarah took your bear." Kevin says, "Yes! She makes me mad. I want my teddy!"

The mother can now handle the situation however she feels best. She might suggest that Kevin ask Sarah nicely to give the bear back, or she might set down an appropriate consequence for Sarah. The important thing is that communication is open. Kevin understands what he was feeling and why he felt that way. The mother does not imply that it was "bad" for him to feel angry. If the mother continues to use the empathic response, Kevin might keep talking about how he feels and why he feels that way. He will feel much better because he has expressed himself, and the mother may be given an important insight into how her children are feeling and relating to one another.

When a child expresses his anger and an adult gives a traditional response —"Don't you dare say you hate your brother!" "That's not true!" "Nice boys never say things like that!" — the response stops the child from communicating further. By clarifying in a non-judgmental way what the child has said, the parent or teacher allows the child to keep expressing himself verbally and to begin to understand his feelings.

Using the empathic response increases the likelihood that a child will find his own solution to a problem. When Dr. Kason's son, Jason, was about eighteen months old, a six-year-old named Jimmy was visiting their home. Jimmy had been given a child's pup tent to play with and was trying to set it up in the family room. Jason was fascinated by the process and thought it was great fun to pull the tent poles down as soon as Jimmy got them set up. Dr. Kason walked into the room just as Jimmy, driven to distraction by the toddler's antics, was screaming, "I hate you! I hate you!" She went to Jimmy and said, "I can see you're really angry and frustrated by the way Jason keeps pulling down your tent poles." Jimmy, quite verbal for his age, said, "Yes. I am *really* frustrated!" Before Dr. Kason could continue, Jimmy said, "You know, I think Jason's too little to know any better, and he'll just keep pulling the poles down because he thinks it's fun. I'm going to go watch TV. He can't wreck *that*!"

When a child can't find the words

An adult can use the empathic response to clarify feelings a child has not verbalized. This usually isn't too difficult. However, if a child is showing signs of being troubled or disturbed, it is a different matter, and the process should be left to properly trained individuals.

I once reprimanded a little boy named Mark for playing dangerously close to a river at a picnic. We had always had a warm and friendly relationship, but the next time he saw me, he pouted, stuck out his lower lip and turned his back on me. I said, "It seems to me you're still angry at me for scolding you the other night. It's okay to feel angry, but I scolded you because you could have been hurt. It doesn't mean that I don't like you." I added, "I hope you get over feeling angry soon so we can have fun together." Mark slowly turned and smiled shyly. The words seemed to wash away the difficulty. Mark had wanted me to know he was angry that our normally trouble-free relationship had been upset, but he hadn't been able to express his emotions in words.

He needed reassurance that our friendship could go on as before in spite of the fact that he had been angry with me and that I had been upset with him. Often when adults see a child pouting or expressing his anger, they tell him to stop. The sullen child will be told rudely to quit sulking. The crying child will be told to grow up or to act like a man. A youngster who is caught lashing out at his brother or damaging something is often jerked away, yelled at, or slapped. He becomes confused about his emotions and begins to suppress them all. Although a child must be stopped when he is involved in a destructive activity and must be punished reasonably when necessary, the process should not stop there. The empathic response can help the child work through the emotions that may have caused the misbehavior in the first place.

Accepting versus encouraging

The adult who uses the empathic response is not encouraging the anger, hatred, hostility, or jealousy the child may be feeling. She is merely accepting the fact that those emotions exist at the moment. This may be a little difficult for some people to do. Many of us have been conditioned to believe that it is very *wrong* to express — or even to feel — negative feelings. Adults, particularly parents, have to overcome this idea if they want to open a channel for communication with their children that will last a lifetime. Again, this does not mean that the adult puts a stamp of approval on the child's negative emotions. Instead, the adult lets the child know his feelings are normal, even though they are not the most desirable ones. If the child has the idea that his emotions are somehow worse than those other people have, he will begin to hide or suppress them. When the adult clarifies the child's emotions for him in an accepting tone, the child begins to understand what he is feeling. After that, he can start to learn how to express his emotions appropriately and discover, with the help of a caring adult, how to work them through.

A child generally does not analyze his feelings, he simply feels them. He may not even be aware that he is having them. Once the adult has clarified and repeated the child's feelings and the child has finished expressing himself, the adult can use the opportunity to suggest ways for the child to handle the situation.

A father might, for example, notice that his daughter is treating her friend in a rough manner and deduce that the reason for this is probably jealousy over the other child's new toy. He might say, "I can see you're angry at your friend. I bet you feel that way because you wish you had a toy like that." If he's right in his clarification his daughter will feel more comfortable about expressing her feelings. She might say, "Yes. I saw that toy on TV and I wanted to have one." The father might then say, "Maybe you could tell your friend that, so he doesn't think you are mad at him." His daughter might reply, "But I want to play with that toy now! And he won't let me!" This opens up the situation, so the father can suggest a solution or help the children come to some solution of their own. He could say, "It looks like a toy two people can play with together. Maybe if you ask him nicely you could do that." Or he might say, "Well, it is *his* toy. How do you think you can work this out?" If the child's old enough she might say, "Well, I guess I can play with my Lego now and see if he'll let me play with it later." Or she might turn to her friend and say, "I'm sorry I pushed you. Could we play together now?"

When you're not sure what the trouble is

It is not always easy to know exactly what a child is feeling. Alisa, a girl I have mentioned before, burst into tears on the third day of school. When I asked her what was wrong she said she didn't know. I took a guess at what was wrong and said, "You know, lots of kids feel very afraid the first week of school, even though they like the school. Sometimes they're afraid they won't do well, even though they want to try real hard. I wonder if you're afraid you won't do well. Could that be why you are crying?" Alisa said it was. I immediately assured her that she didn't need to worry. We could see that she was trying hard and that was what counted at our school. Alisa dried her tears, and in a few moments she was beaming over her work. There were, of course, other reasons Alisa might have been crying. It could have been because she missed her mother or because someone had said something cruel to her on the way to school. If I'd been wrong Alisa would have let me know. When an adult is off base in clarifying a child's emotions, the child will often let her know in no uncertain terms. This has the positive effect of opening up communication, too.

It's all right to cry

Often when our children are expressing negative emotions we don't need to *say* anything at all — we just need to let them know that we are listening and that we empathize with them. We can express this kind of response by saying "I see," or, "Oh," or making a sympathetic sound such as "Hm." This gives the child the opportunity to express his feelings and to keep talking. It's important to remember that when a child is upset or angry, there is a reason for it. He needs the chance to talk to figure out what he is feeling or to give you important information.

I was taking care of Josh, the five-year-old son of a friend and noticed he seemed very troubled. He climbed on my lap and said, "The baby-sitter hit me with the phone yesterday." My instant reaction was to say, "That's crazy. She wouldn't do that!" But I bit my tongue and said, "Hm." Josh continued, "She was talking on the phone, and she was mad at me." Rather than saying, "What did you do to make her mad" I said, "Oh." Josh continued, "When she hung up, she mashed the phone on my arm." He explained that she had hit him before, but he had never told his parents because he had always been doing something he shouldn't when she hit him and he didn't want them to know about the things that he had done. I said, "I see." After a little more talking Josh came to the conclusion, on his own, that he really should tell his parents. I agreed, and Josh told them that evening when they got home.

If I had said something at the beginning of the conversation like, "But that's ridiculous, why would she hit you with a *phone*," it would have stopped the conversation cold. It was important that my responses were supportive but fairly neutral. If I had shouted, "Why, that old witch!" or "She's crazy!" Josh might have exaggerated or become carried away with his story. That would have undermined his credibility and defeated his purpose. What he really wanted — and needed — was to give me information.

Preventing trouble before it begins

The empathic response can often be used to prevent trouble before it begins. Mark's father told me a poignant story that exemplified this. During a birthday celebration for Mark's older brother, Randy, Mark was behaving very badly. He had been causing problems the entire day by reverting to childish behavior and demanding attention in ways his parents thought he had outgrown. No one had thought to help the child express his emotions, even though he obviously felt jealous and left out because of the extra attention his brother was receiving. Mark's acting out escalated. In the evening an adult said, "Mark, you are having trouble cooperating today. You seem really upset about something." Promptly, the child answered, "I am. It's not my birthday and I don't get any hugs." The parents were able to rectify the situation and continue the birthday celebration in peace. Had the child been helped to express his feelings early in the day, a tremendous amount of negative behavior could have been avoided.

It's all right to cry

You can express yourself, too

We shouldn't lose sight of the fact that adults have as legitimate a need to express themselves as children do. Parents and teachers sometimes get the mistaken idea that they need to suppress all their anger and frustration in order to create a warm, loving, positive atmosphere. This is not true. If we are going to be honest with our children, we need to let them know how we feel. When we are angry or upset with something they have done, we should express our feelings in ways that don't threaten the children, make them feel unworthy, or place a load of guilt on their shoulders. A technique that can help us avoid these pitfalls when we want to express our displeasure is to begin our statements with the word *I*: "I get upset when you throw your clothes on the floor. It makes more work for me." "I feel disappointed when you tell me you are going to do something and then you don't follow through." "I get really angry when you get into my makeup case. You have a bag of makeup I've given you. You can play with that, not with mine." "I don't like it at all when you say 'I hate you.' Tell me you're angry in a better way. Maybe then we can solve the problem." Some authors of books on parenting stress this kind of communicating. They call it using "I messages" or "I statements." If you want to learn more about this technique, you can read books by Adele Faber and Elaine Mazlish. ("See our Guide to Books on Parenting.")

There's no script to follow

It is not possible to provide a script for what a parent or teacher should say to a child to help him express himself. The adult must follow her own intuition and rely on her relationship with the child when she wants simple, honest communication to flow between the two of them. It is not always necessary to use a technique like active listening. Dr. Kason and I feel that one of the problems with concepts like active listening and "I messages" is that when they are overused they become contrived and sound false. Real people don't talk like that all the time. Trying to adopt patterns of speech that aren't natural can block a person's sincere, open style of expression. In other words, don't get hung up on a technique or a theory. Use it, by all means, if it helps and is needed, but don't let it keep you from saying what you think when you feel it's right.

There are no pat answers to the question of what is the most appropriate way to express anger and frustration. However, neither Dr. Kason nor I would ever tell a child to stop crying. Instead we would tell him it's all right to cry and that he'll probably feel better afterward. Most psychologists and doctors feel that crying is a healthy, necessary form of expression and that its suppression does great harm. When a child is hitting someone, I stop him and say it's better to yell than hit. In one clinical setting for emotionally disturbed adolescents we suspended a heavy bag for punching in the basement. The kids were encouraged to take their anger out on the bag. They were also encouraged to draw or paint their feelings. This is a technique that can be used successfully by parents. Drawing is especially helpful when a child is having difficulty getting rid of his anger or finding the right words to express it. The parent can say, "Here's a pad and crayons. Can you draw me a picture of how angry you are?" or, "Can you show me how you feel?"

One mother and father I knew gave their son a hammer and boards to pound when he was angry about something. He learned he could take his anger out on an old board rather than on people. Many parents encourage their children to hit a pillow if they are angry. One teacher I worked with had a special pile of clay called "mad clay." When a child was especially angry, he could pound it. This is an excellent idea, because once the child has finished pounding, he can begin to create something out of the clay.

Most mental health professionals agree that it is better to get an emotion out than to hold it in, as long as the method of expression doesn't hurt anyone or destroy something of importance. Ultimately, if a child is encouraged to talk about how he feels, if he discovers that all people have negative emotions at one time or another, and if he realizes that his emotions are an important part of his personality, he will most likely grow into the kind of adult who expresses himself openly, honestly, and appropriately.

Help children express their emotions

- Children need to be able to express their emotions. You can help them learn to do it appropriately.

- Create an atmosphere where a child feels free to talk about his feelings.

- When he expresses negative emotions, simply accept them — don't argue or try to make the child deny his feelings.

- You don't have to approve of negative emotions to accept them.

- Help kids find positive ways to express their feelings and vent their anger. They could pound on a wooden peg set, hit a pillow, pound on some "mad clay," or draw a picture of their anger.

- Never tell a child it's not all right to cry.

- Remember that you have every right to express your feelings and anger, too — just *admit* they're your feelings, don't blame them on the child. Say: "I get absolutely furious when you leave your room in such a mess." Don't say: "You're such a slob. You live like a pig!"

It's all right to cry

How to use the empathic response

❏ Really listen to what the child is saying.

▎ Ben screams, "I hate Samantha, I really hate her!"

❏ Take a second to understand what the child is feeling and why he feels that way.

▎ Mom thinks, Ben must be absolutely furious because Samantha keeps knocking over his blocks.

❏ Clarify the feelings and the reason for them for the child.

▎ Mom says, "I can see you're really angry with Samantha right now because she knocked down your blocks!"

❏ Let the child respond — don't cut him off, argue, or deny.

▎ Ben: "That's right! When she knocked down my tower it made me want to hit her."

▎ Mom: "You're so angry you wanted to hit her."

▎ Ben: "But I'd get in trouble if I hit her. And she's just a baby."

▎ Mom: "Hitting isn't right. And she's just little."

▎ Ben: (much calmer) "She's so little she thinks it's okay to knock down blocks. Maybe I'll wait till later and play with my blocks when she's asleep!"

▎ Mom: "What good thinking, Ben! It really makes me feel great when you handle your feelings like that — have I told you how much I love you today? Come here and give me a big hug!"

Guideline

Expressing emotions is necessary for healthy development. Listen to your kids. Remember that when they are upset they may not be able to say exactly what they mean. Learn to respond in ways that help them understand and express themselves better.

Part Two

Special problems, special solutions

Chapter Twelve

The not so terrible twos

Anyone who lives or works with children knows the early years of a child's life contain certain difficult stages. Probably the most infamous of these is known as the terrible twos. No stage of a child's development is really *terrible*, but this one is certainly trying. Knowing this stage exists isn't enough. In order to deal with it effectively we need to understand why it occurs and to be armed with a supply of what we call "terrible twos antidotes."

It is important to have a general feel for the characteristics of this stage, for no two children go through any developmental period at exactly the same time or in exactly the same way. There are a number of different characteristics that seem to typify the terrible twos. They differ from child to child, but almost all the characteristics seem to be tinged with defiance. The child often refuses to do everything the parents suggest. She often begins to yell and scream. Physically, she is far more easily frustrated and often crankier than she was in the past. She often insists on doing everything herself even if she is not able to, then becomes aggravated by her failure. Struggles often develop between parent and child, especially on occasions when the parent does not have time to allow the child to dress or feed herself. Probably the most shocking thing about this stage is that it seems to develop almost overnight. The cuddly little darling who generally went along with what her mom and dad suggested is suddenly screaming no to almost everything they say. In fact, she sometimes sits there and says no even when no one's saying anything to her.

Some time ago I heard a typical conversation between a two-year-old and his mother.

"Josh, do you want to go to bed?"

"No."

"Are you hungry?"

"No."

"Well, would you like this banana?"

"No," he yelled. Then he grabbed the banana and popped it in his mouth.

Normal developmental behavior

Probably the most reassuring thing about this stage, besides the fact that it doesn't last forever, is that there is a reason for it. It is an important part of the way a child develops into an independent human being.

During the baby's first year she is totally dependent on, and is usually lovingly responsive to, her parents' tender care. In her second year she begins to toddle and talk, but she is still primarily dependent on her parents. Her personality becomes somewhat apparent, but she mimics her parents in speech and action a great deal. In one way what the child is doing during these first two years is gaining the experience she needs to take her first moves toward independence. When she is ready, somewhere around the age of two, she lets go and takes her first *psychological* steps on her own. That the dependent, agreeable baby of yesterday suddenly strikes out for independence is surprising to most parents. The way she does it is often shocking.

There are several reasons this stage has to be so pronounced. The first is that somewhere around the age of two the child begins to develop what is known as autonomy. This is the first step in the development of a self. With autonomy will come independence and individuality. Jean Piaget and other child specialists have noted that a small baby does not really distinguish between herself and her mother. Gradually, she begins to distinguish between herself and others as she becomes aware of her individual wants and desires. Around the time she reaches her second birthday, this realization crystallizes, and she becomes very aware of herself as a separate person. As her ability to communicate with words develops, she distinguishes between "I" or "me" and "you."

Although this process of becoming an individual doesn't complete itself for some years, the two-year-old stage is a turning point. It sems to be a time of rebellion or defiance. But it can be looked at as a kind of overreaction that helps the child distinguish between her own wants and needs and someone else's. In some children it is a relatively mild step, but more often than not it is a turbulent time. The child has experienced two years of almost total dependence. Absolutely everything has been done for her; she has been totally cared for. Suddenly, she can talk, she can move freely, she can feed herself, and she can begin to dress herself. The world opens up for her. As a part of her natural development she grabs at the opportunity to become herself and let her wants be known. Because she was so very dependent in the past, she overdoes her newfound freedom. In this way she defines the boundaries and limits of her personality. The two-year-old is also cranky and defiant because she is undergoing a great amount of inner frustration. She wants to do everything on her own, but she often fails. The things she is learning are complex, and she must sometimes try hundreds of times before she masters a certain task or learns to pronounce a certain word.

These facts all serve to decrease the child's level of tolerance and patience. They are aggravated by the fact that the two-year-old does not get as much attention as she did before. Even though she struggles for self-sufficiency, a part of her wants to hang on to babyhood. Her burning desire to change from a dependent little creature to a self-motivated being is part of her natural development and will triumph in the end. As the child feels more certain of her self and her abilities, it becomes less important for her to assert her independence. As she becomes more competent in language and life skills, the amount of general frustration she feels decreases.

Terrible twos antidotes

In the meantime, understanding why this tumultuous period is occurring should help parents. There are some appropriate antidotes for the battle of the terrible twos. One of the best of these is the "Anti-argument Approach." It consists of remembering that arguing with a child in this trying stage is futile. If she doesn't agree to your polite request after one or two patient tries, she probably isn't going to. Although it's important to give her a chance to agree and do things on her own, when it comes to a conflict of wills it is much better to gently pick the child up and make her do a thing than to have a shouting match. Once, when my little friend Colleen was almost three, she refused to pick up a toy she had deliberately left out. After I asked politely twice, I waited a moment then said, "Here, we'll do it together." I picked her up, carried her to the toy, placed her hand around it and carried both Colleen and toy to the place the toy belonged. I might add, this was not accomplished without a great deal of protest, but it was a better solution than backing down or punishing her for such a small matter.

Another terrific antidote is the "Aha! No Means Yes Approach." The trick is to understand that the child is saying no because she needs to, not because she means it. This helps a parent keep the peace. When Josh, for example, said he didn't want to eat, his mother put the food within his reach, as if he had said he *did* want to eat. If she had become indignant about his attitude and said, "You are going to eat, young man," or tried to force him, Josh would not have eaten.

We can't assume that a two-year-old means yes every time she says no. Since the child is developing her own self and personality at this time, it is important that the parents and day-care workers in her life let her know they respect her feelings and what she says. The problem is to figure out when the child is shouting no out of frustration or for the feeling of power it gives her. When an adult is trying to discover what a two-year-old wants or needs and the child shouts no at every question put to her, it is a good clue that she might have wanted to say yes to at least one of the propositions. Another clue is when the child says no to two questions that require opposite answers, for instance, "Do you want to go to bed?" and, "Do you want to stay up?" It's often a good idea to begin helping the child do the thing you think she wants or needs the most. For example, if an object is in question, like food, clothes, or toys, it's often best to hand the child the thing she most likely wants. If that doesn't work, leave two choices within reach so she can choose.

This leads us to another excellent terrible twos antidote, the "Choice Close." Every good salesperson knows this technique. The secret behind it is to avoid asking yes or no questions. For instance, rather than asking the child if she wants eggs for breakfast, ask her if she'd like to have cereal or eggs. If only toast and eggs are available, the parent might try asking the child which she wants to eat first. The two-year-old may still yell no, but she will tend to act on one of the two choices because she is being given an opportunity to express her own preferences.

Give a two-year-old her own space

A great many conflicts with a two-year-old can be avoided if she is given a place and things of her own that are like those of her parents. As we explained in Chapter Six, these do not need to be elaborate. In the kitchen, for example, the child can be given a drawer or cupboard of her own that is filled with old plastic bowls, pots and pans. She might like a small rake to use when others are working in the yard or little tools to use while she watches someone repair the car. The desire to do everything she sees older people doing — and the conviction that she *can* do it — is one of the strongest feelings a two-year-old has. Toys that imitate the implements adults use can provide her with the means of fulfilling this desire. Her special cupboard in the kitchen or special place in the house where she can keep her things will help give her a sense of identity and a feeling of importance. When the child wants to play with her parents' good dishes, tools, or equipment, the parents can explain she cannot use theirs but she can play with her own. She will often, but not always, accept this alternative without a fuss. It works far better than simply telling the child that she cannot do something.

The two-year-old stage is sometimes a trying time for parents or day-care workers, but it is also a trying time for the child. She wavers uncertainly between the security of babyhood and the excitement of childhood. She must store away tremendous amounts of information and master difficult tasks. Probably most frustrating of all, she has a powerful desire to do everything all by herself, yet she is not even close to having the ability she needs to accomplish these tasks. Armed with this understanding, adults can structure their child's environment to minimize conflict and increase her confidence and feelings of self-worth. This stage, for all its drawbacks, is one of the most exciting to watch, as the child develops her ability to communicate, reveals more of her unique personality, and relates with unbounded enthusiasm to the world around her.

Often learning about a particular developmental stage can help you be more tolerant and understanding of a child's behavior. In *Dr. Mom*, Marianne Neifert gives a good overview of each of the developmental stages. If you want detailed information, read the books by Louise Ames and Frances Ilg, from the Gesell Institute. (See our Guide to Books on Parenting.)

Chapter Thirteen

School blues

A child's attitude toward life is colored by the way he feels about himself in school. Very few children who have difficulty with schoolwork are happy in any area of their lives. The discouragement the child feels about failing in school hangs like a cloud over all his other activities. Even during the summer holidays, the mere thought of school will dampen the most exciting time. On weekends, depressing thoughts about Monday morning are never far from the surface. When a parent sees a child in such a condition, she may desperately want to help but she might have no idea what to do. There are, however, many positive approaches a parent can take to help a child overcome school failure.

One of the most important things for the parent to do is to try to discover why the child is having trouble. It may shock most parents to discover that very little school failure is caused by lack of intelligence. If a child has always seemed bright around the house and has seemed to pick things up quickly, he probably has all the intelligence necessary to succeed in school. Even if he hasn't seemed quick or particularly bright, he may be quite intelligent, and he may be failing around the house for the same reason he's "failing" in school. Children fail for a variety of reasons.

Failing for attention

One of the main reasons children fail in school is that they have a desperate need for attention. A child often decides subconsciously that if he can't be a stunning success, he might as well be a stunning failure. Very early in life he may learn that his mediocre achievements don't net him anything. He has seen that when he does something unusually well he receives praise and attention, but that when he does something only fairly well or in an average manner he gets no attention all. He has probably also discovered that when he does something very poorly, he also receives a great deal of attention. And even though it's negative attention it's better than no recognition at all. Thus, a child who needs more attention may begin to fail in order to get attention. Remember, attention takes many forms: physical affection, recognition, praise, time for talking, time for playing, or even a general kind of affirmation of a child's existence and importance. Parents may *love* their child a great deal, but still not be giving him the type of feedback he needs. They might also, in spite of their best intentions, not be giving enough. Children differ tremendously in how much acknowledgment they need. Parents must be sensitive to this and respond accordingly.

A child I met while teaching in Europe provides an example of how the failure-for-attention process works. This child wanted time with his father more than anything else in the world.

The boy was about thirteen years old when I met him. He was the son of a Yugoslavian sea captain, who spent almost all his time at sea. The father was a very intelligent man. He spoke the languages of the seven countries he regularly traveled to with ease, and his fluency had given him certain advantages in life. He was adamant that his son do well in foreign-language classes. (It is not uncommon for a child in the European school system to be studying three languages at a time.)

The boy, who was an electronic wizard, did well in all his subjects until his preteen years.

It was the father's custom to come home after weeks or months at sea, greet his family and lose himself in the local newspaper to catch up on news and relax. He spent almost no time communicating with his son. He reasoned that he was home and that was good enough. If the boy showed him his report card, he would pat the child on the head and tell him to run along and play. A major change in this pattern occurred one day when the son handed the father a report card on which the child's mark in English was lower than the rest. The father took note of this fact, spent some time discussing the importance of learning English to the child and told him that he must improve his work.

It should come as no surprise that when the father returned after his next trip, the boy handed him a report card with a failing mark in English. The father spent at least an hour lecturing and scolding the boy. This was the most attention the child had received from his father at one time. On the father's next home visit the child had not only failed English, but was also doing poorly in French, German, and his native language, Croatian.

The story of the captain and his son is a typical one. The father was a well-meaning and loving man. He wanted the boy to succeed for his own good and would never have intentionally done anything to hold the child back in life. However, that is exactly what he was doing.

Competition and comparison with siblings

Some children fail because they are competing with their brothers and sisters. This is often tied in with the need for attention. It generally occurs when a child of average ability in school sees someone in his family doing extremely well and getting praise for it. He may then begin to strive to do just as well. If he falls short, he may become discouraged about his own ability. If his average work doesn't get praise, he may give up and begin to fail. He will undoubtedly get negative attention for failing, and this may satisfy his need to be noticed by his parents.

An example of how this occurs was played out in detail in a family I knew with two sons. When the oldest boy, Larry, began school, he did above-average work for two years. During his third year of school, his younger brother, Keith, started grade one and began to bring home outstanding report cards. Larry's marks dropped suddenly and drastically while Keith continued to do well. Unfortunately for the two boys, no one in the family made a connection between Keith's success and Larry's failure. Larry left high school before graduation; Keith went to university. I had known the boys for some time, and it seemed obvious to me that Larry had every bit as much potential as Keith. Had someone in the family or school system recognized this, life could have been made much simpler for both boys. Larry suffered because he failed, and Keith felt the effects of the strain their differences put on their relationship.

The need for attention was only part of the problem. The roots of Larry's school failure probably began before he lost interest in school, and could probably be traced to Keith's birth or the time when he began to toddle and talk. I learned that an obvious comparison had always been made between the boys. The mother had a preference for Keith the moment he was born: from that time on he was considered the cuter and smarter baby. Larry may have carried these subconscious memories into his school years. As long as he was the only one in school, he received attention for his progress. He may have worried about what would happen when Keith started school. In his fantasy world he may have often feared that his brother would do better and that he would lose the only favored position he had ever held. At the first hint that this was happening, he may have panicked and given up. Once he had failed, for whatever reason, and discovered that this brought him attention, he settled into the only role he felt he could fulfill.

Many parents handle the difference in their children's abilities in positive ways. One of these involves focusing on each child's strengths. Another is recognizing or validating their individual differences from early childhood. My best friend from childhood and her husband have done a beautiful job of this. They have four handsome, healthy boys with extremely different personalities, tastes, and abilities. Each time I have visited them over the years, I have been amazed at how little competition there is among the brothers. Each has found his particular niche — his special area for success and achievement. The oldest is an academic whiz who is quite determined to go into law. The second is an artist who gets a great deal of recognition at home and at school for his ability to draw cartoons. The third, who does fairly well in school but who does not have the unusual academic or artistic abilities of his older brothers, is a "people person." He has an outstanding ability to make friends and get along with others. The youngest boy has a tremendous interest in sports and athletics. The parents certainly never tried to channel any of the boys into any particular area, but they did help each child build his feelings of self-esteem on his own individual strengths. At the same time, no one boy has ever been pushed to live up to the level set by another. This is particularly clear in the case of the third son. Many parents, faced with one child who is not so outstanding in obvious ways as another, forget to take the time to discover the ways in which he is outstanding. My friends, however, recognized the gift of being a "people person" in their son and gave it the acknowledgment it deserved. This helped him develop self-esteem; consequently, he doesn't worry that one brother might be smarter or another more talented. So he doesn't try to compete — beginning what would inevitably be a cycle of failure. He has his own strengths. And he knows it.

Poor self-image

Some children fail in school because of their attitudes about themselves; they fail because they think they are going to fail. Psychologists have called this the "self-fulfilling prophecy" and have done extensive research on it. They have found that when a child thinks he is stupid, he will behave as if he is; when he is convinced he can't succeed, he won't.

A woman I knew, Tina, had a terrible image of herself. When she made mistakes as a child her father usually said things like, "You dumb brat," "You stupid idiot," and, "Don't you have a brain in your head?" Tina went through grade school making mediocre grades, which her father disparaged. When she reached the sixth grade, however, and the work became more difficult, she began to fail. She often called herself stupid and was quite convinced that she was not smart enough to do schoolwork. After the summer of her seventh grade, a relative came to visit. This relative knew nothing of Tina's rocky school history. Impressed by the child's understanding of politics and her grasp of world events, the relative repeatedly complimented Tina on her brightness and obvious intelligence. Stunned, Tina returned to school with a new image of herself. In grade eight her marks were all high. She went on to do honors work in high school and university, and has often remarked what a tremendous difference the relative made in her life.

Many children are not as fortunate as Tina. They suffer from the misconception that they are inadequate or unintelligent for their entire lives. These ideas cause school failure. The failure then reinforces the child's negative feelings about himself. This needless cycle continues for thousands of children who have adequate intelligence and yet have never been given a chance to discover it.

Other reasons children fail

Problems in the home are another factor that can bring about school failure. A child often becomes distraught when there have been fights, arguments, or scenes in his home. In school he is unable to concentrate because the difficulties in his home are playing on his mind. The more these difficulties create an aura of insecurity in his life, the less able he will be to focus his attention on school. When a child's home is insecure, the child must fight for psychological survival. The pressing internal needs he has far outweigh the importance of anything he might be learning in school. Once his home difficulties bring about failure at school, his failure may causie even more friction in the home.

School failure is also brought about by the inadequacy of schools. There is often no time for the regular classroom teacher to help the stumbling, introverted, or troubled child. The emphasis placed on Caucasian, middle-class values is often totally irrelevant to a child from a different cultural background. A child may have a specific learning disability or emotional problem that the regular classroom teacher doesn't recognize. Failure is sometimes caused by the school system's emphasis on visual learning; some children learn better through listening and using their other senses than through reading. Some of these specialized difficulties are discussed in later chapters.

Drugs and alcohol can also cause a child to fail in school. It is impossible for a child to attend to the business of learning when his thinking is impaired by intoxicants. Tragically, the number of children who are using drugs is far higher than the number of children parents *think* are using drugs. Often unsuspecting parents don't wake up until far too much damage has been done. Signs that a child may be using drugs include: a drop in school performance; a sudden change in personality, habits, or friends; a general apathy and lack of interest; a noticeable secretiveness or isolation from the rest of the family;

deterioration in personal care or hygiene; changes in patterns of sleeping and waking or the amount of time spent away from home; a decrease in appetite; glassy eyes or unusually dilated or constricted pupils. Parents should take note of liquor missing from bottles and of any drug-related paraphernalia — such as pipes and roach clips — they find in a child's room. Missing money, the suspicion that the child is stealing, and unaccountable expenses can also be clues to drug abuse: kids have to pay for the drugs somehow.

Anytime there is a sudden change in school performance, parents should consider a medical checkup for their child. The problem could be related to drug or alcohol abuse or any of a number of other medical problems, including a difficulty with sight or hearing. A family physician may also spot an emotional or psychological difficulty the parents are not aware of.

There are many things a warmhearted adult can do to help a failing child improve his standing at school.

Positive reinforcement can help

If a child is failing in order to get attention, the parents must recognize why the child behaves this way. They should evaluate how and when they give attention to the child. They usually find they make far more to-do about bad grades than about his good ones. They may discover that the only time their child is singled out and given their undivided attention is when he hands them a terrible report card. Once the parents realize the child needs attention, they can begin to break the child's pattern of failure by placing more attention on the good work the child is doing.

It is not always easy to place more attention on a child's good work than his poor work, especially if the child is failing across the board. However, every child does some things well. The parent must find those things and compliment them. She can also encourage the child to show her his homework. When she looks the pages over she can make sincere, positive comments, such as, "Look at these three sentences! They are very good. You've used the vocabulary words correctly, and the writing is easy to read!" or, "You got every multiplication problem in the first three rows correct. That's a big improvement." Always look for improvement and focus on it. It does not matter if the work is not up to grade level or does not meet the highest standards — if it is the best your child can do or if it is better than his past work, praise him. The child needs to hear your praise.

The parent continues to make positive comments on the child's work every day until the child brings home his next report card. On that day, she makes sure she spends as much — if not more — time discussing the report card with the child as she did before. Only this time she should discuss the positive aspects of the card. If the child was singled out and scolded for a lengthy amount of time for his poor marks in the past, he should be singled out and praised for the same amount of time. If there is no improvement in grades, the parent can talk about all the progress she has seen the child making or all the effort she has seen him putting out. The parent should convey encouragement and understanding. If any of the child's marks have improved, his good work in these areas should be emphasized. The poor marks should be given as little attention as possible.

The child's work will begin to improve as his need for attention is being satisfied in a positive way. As this process is taking place, the parent will need to continually praise and give attention to the child's progress. It may take a child a long time to catch up, especially if he's in a crowded classroom where the teacher has little time to attend to individual needs. The child may be sincerely striving to do better, but have so many gaps in his learning that he doesn't know how to begin. In this case a little private tutoring might help the child a great deal and be well worth the expense.

The Yugoslavian sea captain applied this positive attitude to his son's work, and the boy made stunning progress in a very short time. The father also realized how much his adolescent son needed him and began to spend more time at home.

For children who seem to be failing because of competition with an outstanding brother or sister the helping process is much the same. The parents must focus positive attention on whatever the child does well and give as little attention as possible to his failing work. They must be careful to give an equal amount of praise and affection to both children, regardless of their differences in ability and talent.

Every child has some strong point, and parents can build the confidence of their failing child by helping him discover what his special abilities are.

Combating low self-esteem

When low self-esteem or a negative attitude about himself is contributing to a child's failure at school, parents will find they can, in general, help their child improve his self-image by treating him in the positive, respectful ways we talk about throughout this book. There are also more specific approaches. One is to help a child become aware of the negative ideas he has about himself, and help him replace them with positive ones. Children with negative self-images are often quite verbal about the things they believe are wrong with them. They can often be heard saying things like: "I'm so stupid," "I can't do that, I'm not smart enough," or, "I can't do anything right." These comments sometimes call for parents to encourage deeper communicating by using the empathic response technique discussed in Chapter Eleven. This gives the parents an opportunity to supply the child with information that contradicts his negative ideas. After the child has expressed his feelings about being stupid, the parent might say, "Remember the way you fixed the radio last week? That took good thinking."

It isn't always necessary to try to involve the child in a lengthy discussion about his feelings. A straightforward, heartfelt response that gives the child your opinion can help him, too: "Hey, *I* think you're a pretty smart kid!" But it's a good idea to add specifics: "You figured out what was wrong with your bike yesterday and fixed it by yourself. That took a kind of smarts I don't have." There is also a lot of truth in old homilies like, "Nobody's good at everything." Children can adjust to the fact that they have weaknesses; they just need to know they have strengths to build on.

It is also important to keep in mind that children often learn these negative attitudes about themselves from their parents. Tina was a good example of this. Her parents told her she was stupid and that she couldn't do anything right. This created her low self-esteem and her belief that she was unintelligent and incapable. Parents who tell their children things like this have to be honest enough with themselves to admit their mistakes. They have to eliminate negative labels, even those said partly in jest, like, "You nitwit" and, "Dummy!" They must learn to focus on the many intelligent things the child does every day.

Many children who have problems in school need to have the clever things they do pointed out to them again and again. Still, as we've said before, the parent has to be careful not to exaggerate or overdo the praise. If praise is not sincere, the child will sense it. When it's extremely difficult to compliment a child's work at a certain level, he should be given simpler things to do that he can succeed at. In this way the parent can sincerely praise the child's work and help him build his self-confidence so that he can move on to more difficult tasks.

Making the best of family problems

When parents think difficulties in the home are contributing to a child's problems in school, there are a few things they can do to help. The first is to discover whether they have been trying to hide their difficulties from the child. Many parents do not realize that it is almost impossible to keep serious marital problems from an intuitive, sensitive child. Children can sense a strained atmosphere, even when arguments are not held in front of them. When no one admits that a difficult situation exists, the child has no way to deal with it. He has to pretend there's no problem, even though he knows there is. He can't approach anyone about his fears, since there isn't supposed to be anything to be afraid of. All these factors cause him to hold his worries in and keep them to himself. Since he has no release for them, they weigh heavily on his mind and become greatly exaggerated. These concerns can begin to occupy a majority of his time and blot out whatever he is supposed to be learning.

One solution to this difficulty may be for the parents to be more honest and open, so the child knows where he stands. What he may have interpreted as imminent disaster in his home might be the growing pains of the marriage, and the child can be helped to understand.

If the end of the marriage is at hand, a child will need to know the truth at some point. Counseling may be required for the child who has already begun to show his distress by developing problems in school. Until he has a grasp of the situation, his mind will be flooded with questions about who he will live with, what will happen to his house, and how often he will see the other parent. When these questions are answered — and he has had help adjusting — it will be easier for him to focus his attention on his schoolwork.

Parents can also help a child through this rocky period by telling the child's teacher, so she can be prepared to assist the child.

When more help is needed

There are children who, because of brain damage or other extreme factors, are less able to learn. Fortunately, such children are being recognized and helped by professionals at an earlier and earlier age. If parents feel their child isn't getting the help he needs within the school system, they can go to community and government agencies to find specialists who will advise them. Even children with severe problems may show astounding progress when treated with praise and positive attention in the home.

Each reason for school failure has been considered here as if it were a separate entity. However, more often than not, children fail because of a combination of reasons. It is only when they are treated with love, care, and understanding in terms of their academic development that they will develop the confidence and self-esteem they need to become loving, satisfied adults.

Chapter Fourteen

Half a family
— a whole child

A child suffers greatly with the loss of a parent, whether it is from divorce, separation, or death. Ideally, a child grows up in the presence of both a mother and a father. This provides the child with role models, helps her develop her sexual identity, and helps her grow into a balanced adult who is able to give and receive love easily. But it is also possible for a single parent to raise emotionally healthy and well-adjusted children.

The loss of one parent raises complex questions that require more attention than we are able to provide here. But we can present a few insights into how some of the strain a child is bound to feel can be alleviated. We can encourage single parents to feel good about looking for help if it's needed. Some single parents are hesitant about getting help. They shouldn't be. Family doctors, psychologists, and friends who've lived through the experience can often offer good advice, and there is a great deal of good literature on the subject.

Close to half the marriages in North America end in divorce. It's clear we don't take the marriage vows as seriously as our grandparents did; there's also probably some truth to the platitudes, "Nowadays people use divorce as an easy way out," and, "It ought to be as hard to get married as it is to get divorced." Still, if you take the time to think about most of the couples you know who have been divorced, you'll find they are people who took their original commitment seriously and, especially if there were children involved, did everything they could to make the marriage work.

Most people agree that couples should make an extraordinary effort to work out their differences when there are children involved. But some differences really are irreconcilable, and there can be a danger in staying together for the children. The conflict created in such a situation can be much harder on the children than living with only one parent might be. Children are often perceptive enough to see this even at an early age. I once heard an eight-year-old say, "I wish Mommy and Daddy would get a divorce, then it wouldn't be so awful around here." One of the worst things parents can do in such a situation is stay together and say they are doing it for the children. This lays a tremendous burden of guilt on the child. Each time the parents fight, the children feel personally responsible and blame themselves for the unhappiness.

When a single-parent family is created — either through divorce or through the death of a parent — many things can be done to make it easier on the child. One of these is realizing that the child will experience feelings of grief, guilt, and rage, and will want to blame someone for her situation. A parent needs to understand what's going on in the child's mind, to accept her feelings and help her learn to express them appropriately.

Another important role of the single parent is to provide his child with opportunities to identify with people of the same sex as the missing partner. Also, in the case of divorce, both parents need become aware of the devious games separated people can begin to play — sometimes unwittingly, but always at the child's expense.

Common emotions

Most of us expect a child who has lost a parent to feel sad and bereft, but many people are surprised to learn a child can also feel a great deal of guilt. The first step in combating this is to be honest with the child about what happened, so the child understands Daddy or Mommy did not leave or die *because of her.* This sounds so obvious it is hard for some of us to understand how a child could possibly imagine she caused one of her parents to leave. But children *do* think this, and telling them it is not so once is not enough; most children need to be repeatedly reassured. A young child I know was done untold harm by a mother who told him, after the father deserted them, "Daddy doesn't love *us* any more." Although the mother may have been telling the truth, her real purpose was a vain attempt to fill her own emptiness by drawing her child into the misery. The child is now grown but still remembers his mother's words clearly. He was filled with guilt. In his childlike way of thinking, the important factor in the *us* was *him*: Daddy didn't love him anymore, so Daddy went away; he must have been a very bad boy to drive Daddy away. It took years of introspection and counseling before he came to terms with the situation.

The reason a child needs to understand that the parents are not separating because of her is a complex one. The same thing holds true for children who have lost a parent through death. Apart from the obvious reason that no child should have to endure such a feeling of rejection, there is a much deeper underlying factor. As part of their sexual development, all children fantasize about having the parent of the opposite sex "all to themselves." In their daydreams they see Mommy or Daddy conveniently out of the picture and dream of being the little man or woman of the house. According to Freudian theory, this is part of a child's natural development. It is necessary for her to play out these roles in her dreamworld in order for her to function in relationships in later years. In addition to this, some young children of both sexes fantasize to some extent about having Mommy all to themselves, since when Daddy comes home in the evening, they no longer receive Mommy's undivided attention. These fantasies are common in different degrees for three- to six-year-olds, and then again, on a more sophisticated level, for adolescents.

The complicating factor comes when one of these fantasies becomes real through divorce, separation, or death. The child has usually not verbalized any of the fantasies, which have remained part of her inner, secret world — a world which is very real to her. This inner world of magic and make-believe is so real to her that she assumes it has power. She sometimes believes that her wishing has driven the parent away. The child is very unlikely to express these fears. It is very important, therefore, for the parent to let the child know that her feelings had no effect on the termination of the relationship. This can be done very easily with words such as, "You know sometimes little boys or girls wish they had Mommy all to themselves, but this can't make Daddy go away. Daddy went away because he and I couldn't get along, and we knew the home would be happier this way." If it is appropriate, the mother or father could add that they know the other parent misses the child very much. Again, these things may have to be repeated, especially if there is any indication that the child feels guilty over the father's or mother's absence.

The child may also feel tremendous hostility and anger at the loss of a parent. Surprisingly enough, this anger will tend to be directed at the parent who is still in the home. It's not uncommon for a child to flip back and forth, in her mind, between blaming herself and blaming the remaining parent. An angry, frustrated child will often yell things like, "I hate you. You made Daddy go away." Once, in a play-therapy situation, I watched a six-and-a-half-year-old girl act out the story of her father leaving the home with little dolls. Throughout the entire session, she called the male doll "Daddy" and the female doll "the bad wife." It became clear that she knew her mother was a good mommy, so she reasoned Daddy must have gone away because Mommy was a bad wife. In her mind, the guilt lay with her mother. Eventually, she came to understand the reasons the marriage hadn't worked. Her father was able to be especially helpful in this process by telling the child — more than once — how her mother had, indeed, been a good wife, but that they had not made a good husband and wife together. None of this would have been resolved if the child had not been able to express her thoughts or get her feelings out in the open.

Thus, instead of admonishing the child for negative feelings and statements, the parents need to help her express them. This is a hard thing to do. When a child screams, "I hate you," or, "It's your stupid fault Mommy went away," our natural reaction is to say, "Don't let me *ever* hear you say that again!" Still, it can help if the parent understands that the child's scope is small; children tend to see the world in terms of themselves, first and foremost. They see the immediate disadvantages to themselves in a divorce, rather than the long-range positive effect of living in a more peaceful home. They feel betrayed by the loss of a parent. To some extent their anger is justified. Although it's not pleasant to think a child has these feelings, she does. Scolding her will only make her bury them deeper in her inner world, where they will eat at her for years. We are not saying that anger and hostility should be encouraged, but they should be accepted and expressed and gotten rid of using the methods discussed in Chapter Eleven. When this is done with warmth and compassion, the child will know her true feelings are understood and accepted. Even though they aren't the best feelings, she will be able to work them out rather than suppress them. This does not mean that the child of a single parent should be allowed to get away with misbehavior. There may be times, especially early on, when a child misbehaves more than usual because of the turbulent emotions she's feeling. Still limits and consequences should remain as close to the norm as possible.

Games ex-partners play

There are several destructive games separated parents sometimes play. One of the worst is when one or both of them give privileges or gifts in order to win the child's approval. One parent will sometimes use the child's favor or preference as a tool against the other parent. Many single parents find themselves involved in this deceitful game without realizing it. It is quite easy for the parent who is no longer living at home to fall into this trap. The weekends and vacations when this parent has the children become a kind of party, where one special event follows the other, candy, and other treats are allowed without restriction, and the children are never made to do chores.

Time spent with this parent becomes something that isn't part of the real world. This is harmful enough, but it's worse when the "weekend" parent intentionally fosters this kind of environment so the children will like him best or so he can hurt the other parent with comments like, "See, the kids can't even stand you," and, "The kids would rather be with me — and no wonder." This kind of petty behavior occurs far more frequently than we would imagine among sane, responsible adults. Tragically, no matter how hard one parent tries to hurt the other in this way, it is the children who are ultimately hurt. When a weekend parent finally realizes what he's doing, he must stop. If his feelings of anger and hostility toward the other parent are so great that he cannot break the cycle on his own, he needs to seek out professional help. This game is terribly destructive.

There is not much the parent who has the child most of the time can do if he discovers the other parent is trying to win the child over with excessive gifts or privileges during visiting times. Ideally, this parent should be able to communicate his concern about the child's welfare and security to the other parent. Unfortunately, this ideal is often not possible. If nothing can be done to change the situation the parent at home must stick to his guns and keep the limits and privileges at home consistent. This is not always easy to do, especially when a child comes home after a visit and says, "Mommy doesn't make me do the dishes at her house!" or, "Mommy lets me go to the show whenever I want."

It is difficult not to give in. It hurts us to think a child likes the other parent better or enjoys visiting more than being at home. This can create a tremendous pressure on the home parent and make him think he should relax the rules around the house. A friend of mine who was going through a divorce provided an example of this one day when she told me, "I'm making the boys clean their room today. They sure are unhappy about it. They've been with their dad for a week over the holidays and he does nothing but Santa Claus kind of stuff with them. You know, maybe I should let up on them and they'd be happier around here."

It is important for a parent who finds himself in this situation to remember, in spite of what a child says when she is trying to get her own way or get out of doing household chores, that she really does want consistency and limits. And she does not really want excessive gifts. They trouble her or make her feel uneasy because they aren't being given at customary times. She also senses that they are being given insincerely. Even though it is often difficult, the parent who is striving to keep the home life as normal as possible must stick to his guns. The knowledge that this is really what a child wants and needs — regardless of what he says — might make life a little easier.

Another game separated parents need to avoid is the degradation of the other parent in front of the child. Dr. Kason and I have seen fairly well-adjusted children develop serious emotional problems when their separated parents tried to tear each other down in the child's eyes. A colleague of mine told me about how this affected her son. She was divorced many years ago, when her son was seven. The son remained with his father and her daughter went with her. She did not want to be separated from the boy, but the boy's paternal grandparents placed a tremendous amount of pressure on her and convinced her it would be the best thing she could do for him. She finally agreed.

The boy's father immediately took his son and moved out of town. He told the boy his mother had abandoned him and that she had become a prostitute. He tore up all the letters the mother wrote to the boy, destroyed the gifts she sent, and whenever she called he told her the boy wasn't home. When she was finally able to contact the boy, his mind was so poisoned against her that he wouldn't speak to her. In spite of this, she continued to make efforts. Finally, when the boy was about sixteen — and learned that his mother was a teacher, not a prostitute — he agreed to see her. Since then the mother and son have made progress in establishing a relationship. But the son, now a man in his late twenties, has been unable to form any lasting relationships with women. He is in intensive psychotherapy in an attempt to deal with his deep-seated fear of being abandoned by women. Even though he now knows his mother didn't abandon him, the scars created by what his father told him are real, and he is having a hard time coming to terms with his fears.

One parent's tearing down of the other can backfire. Many children will end up despising the mother if she told them how terrible their father was — regardless of whether the things she said were true. We are not suggesting one parent try to lie or cover up for the other, but a parent shouldn't degrade the other or tell the truth in a cruel manner. In general the wisest path for a single parent seems to be the one on which he strives to forgive, forget, and treat his ex-partner with as much understanding and respect as he can muster in front of the children.

Role models

It has long been held that single parents do a great service to their children by providing them with role models who are the same sex as the missing parent. This might involve seeking out a new relationship — when the time is right — or finding members of the family or community who are available to serve as male or female models for the child. Two common misconceptions need to be pointed out here. First, children of both sexes need to be provided with role models of the same sex as the missing parent. In other words, if a father is missing, the girls and the boys in the family will need masculine role models. Many people tend to think that a boy needs to be around a male role model or that a girl needs to be around a female role model, but this is only a partial truth. Second, role models need to be adults. Other children don't work in this capacity.

Single parents are sometimes hesitant to ask, but close friends of the family or relatives are often more than willing to spend time with children who need them. If no one suitable close to the family exists, there are teachers, ministers, and members of other community organizations who may help. There are clubs like Girl Guides and Boy Scouts, where the group leaders often provide good models. Boys and girls will benefit from organizations where they can learn to camp, fish, sew, or participate in any kind of activity the missing parent might have been skilled in. Many communities offer volunteer big-brother or big-sister organizations.

Although these alternatives may not prove to be as good as a solid two-parent home, they are certainly better than a second broken home. Too many single parents are tempted to rush into second marriages before the time is right just to provide a mother or father for their children. Unfortunately, in their eagerness, these well-meaning single parents sometimes go into marriage without going over the basic ground rules with the new partner. It is imperative that the new partner is willing to work on accepting and loving the children as his own. He must also agree with the way the children are being raised; this is assuming, of course, that they are being raised properly. If the partner does not accept the children or the way they are being raised, things may proceed smoothly for a while, but the peace cannot last. Entering into a second marriage without enough foresight can be tragic. The children are caught in the middle and can easily end up feeling responsible for the failure of the second marriage and losing their faith that any marriage could ever work.

The issues involved in being a single parent and in dealing with the emotional upheaval children experience at the loss of or separation from a parent are complex. While we have touched on a few of the important concerns in this chapter, single parents may want to read about the subject. Two good books are *Helping Children Cope with Separation and Loss* by Claudia Jewett and *How To Single Parent* by Fitzhugh Dodson. (See our Guide to Books on Parenting.)

Being a single parent has to be one of the most difficult jobs in the world, but it is one that can be done — and done well. Thousands of children from single-parent families who are growing up to be well-rounded, well-adjusted adults are living proof.

Chapter Fifteen

Slow child in a fast world

A great many children need special help and special education. Among them are children with learning disabilities, emotional problems, and various degrees of mental retardation. According to some statistics, as many as two out of every ten children fall into one of these categories. This means the lives of many people are touched by children with special needs. Even if you do not have a child with one of these difficulties in your family, you and your children will almost certainly be coming in contact with them. This is especially true now that the trend in education is to integrate special-needs children into the regular classroom instead of isolating them in special-education classes. Since being better informed can help you and your children relate more positively to children with special needs, Dr. Kason and I provide an overview of the most common problems in the next three chapters. In this chapter we look at the question of mental retardation. But before we go on we need to discuss the term mental retardation itself. A number of associations that deal with this problem have made an effort, in the past few years, to eliminate some of the prejudice against people who have this disability by changing the terminology involved. In a number of places the public is now being urged to use the term "people with developmental handicaps" rather than "the mentally retarded." In some areas the use of the term "handicaps" in any context is considered disrespectful and so the phrase "persons with developmental disabilities" is used. While Dr. Kason and I are extremely supportive of any movement to reduce prejudice against any special needs child, we have chosen to use the term mental retardation in this chapter since there is still considerable regional controversy over the most acceptable term. Also, mental retardation is the term accepted by the American Association for the Mentally Retarded and by the American Psychiatric Association.

Unfortunately, misunderstandings about people with mental retardation are pervasive in our society. When I was in graduate school I conducted a survey on people's attitudes about mental retardation. The most significant findings came from the last two questions on the questionnaire. "Would you be afraid if you saw someone you thought was a retarded person walking toward you on the street?" Ninety percent of the those questioned said no. "Do you think most people would be?" Ninety percent said yes!

Because of certain things we know about the way people answer questionnaires, we can assume that most people who said *they* wouldn't be afraid but that others would actually be frightened by a retarded person. The study also showed that these people had a very stereotypical idea of what a retarded person would look like in spite of the fact that — with the exception of certain syndromes that affect appearance as well as mental capacity — most people who are mentally retarded look just like anyone else.

The tremendous efforts made by organizations to educate the public and by wonderful programs like the Special Olympics have improved people's understanding of mental retardation in the past decade. But stereotypes and groundless fears still exist. The purpose of this chapter is to provide some information on what mental retardation is, what causes it and how it is frequently mistaken for something else. We hope this information will dissolve any misconceptions or fears you might have about retardation so you can help your child remain free from them. He will then be able to learn to appreciate, enjoy, and learn from the retarded children he comes in contact with.

What causes mental retardation?

One of the most startling facts about mental retardation is that, in a great many cases, medical and educational experts don't know what causes it. In other cases there are clearly identifiable traumatic, chromosomal, or genetic causes. The term *traumatic* refers to physical damage to the brain caused by something like a blow to the head or a lack of oxygen. This is generally referred to as *brain damage*, and although the term is used loosely by many people, it accounts for only a small percentage of cases of mental retardation. A trauma to the brain can occur before, during, or after birth. Drugs, radiation, and infection are other causes of brain damage. It is important to note that a child can have brain damage and not be affected mentally. Depending on the seriousness of the trauma and the area of the brain it has affected, the resulting problem may be physical rather than mental. Cerebral palsy is an example of this. Although children with this condition have varying degrees of difficulty with motor coordination and the control of their limbs, few are mentally retarded. In other words, they have normal intelligence levels. For years, children with CP were thought to be retarded because many of them did not have enough muscle control to learn to speak or communicate. Today, however, computers and a wonderful invention called the Bliss Symbol Board — which the child with cerebral palsy can use to express his thoughts, feelings and desires — have opened up new worlds for these children and have shown us how wrong we were.

Chromosomal abnormalities cause certain types of retardation. The most common is Down's syndrome. Down's syndrome children were once called "mongoloids," a name derived from certain physical characteristics most Down's syndrome children have, including broad, flat faces, almond-shaped eyes, and stocky builds. Scientists have discovered that all people who suffer from Down's syndrome have an extra chromosome connected to the twenty-first pair of chromosomes. While scientists know how this abnormality in the genetic makeup occurs, they are not always certain of why it happens. One significant factor is the age of the parents. Although people of any age can conceive a Down's syndrome child, the risk increases with maternal age and increases more rapidly the older a woman becomes. The father's age is also a factor, with significantly more Down's syndrome babies being born to fathers older than fifty.

Other kinds of retardation for which physical causes can be found have to do with other chromosomal abnormalities or with irregularities in the way certain glands, such as the pituitary and the thyroid, function. Heredity can also be a factor in the cause of mental retardation.

Some children are born with certain syndromes — a group of recognizable characteristics — that include retardation. In some cases, even though scientists and doctors have identified the syndrome, they have not yet found the cause.

When no cause can be found

Many explanations have been offered as to what the origin might be of those cases of retardation for which no physical cause can be found. One possibility is lack of environmental stimulation. Another is poor nutrition. Some doctors feel that many children with retardation may have some kind of brain damage that we cannot yet identify. Some children who are labeled retarded may simply not be living up to their potential. In other words, they act retarded or function as if they are retarded, when they actually have average or above-average intelligence. This may be their way of coping with emotional problems, fear, or lack of attention. It is also possible that they have some undiagnosed physical problem, such as a vision or hearing impairment, which hinders their learning. Other children may think so poorly of themselves because of how they have been treated that they never realize they are smart enough or good enough to learn.

In other cases, children may be labeled mentally retarded when they have language problems or lack communication skills. This happens to many children who come from different cultures or speak a different language. Striking examples of this have been found across North America. I had the opportunity several years ago of working in the special-education system in Albuquerque, New Mexico. There, as many as ninety percent of the children enrolled in special-education classes were Mexican-American or native Americans. It has only been in the past decade and a half that educators have begun to listen to the people who have claimed that it isn't possible for so many children in a certain cultural group to be retarded. Since then it has been found that most of these children have difficulties in school because they have not learned English. Similar problems have occurred because of cultural differences. Some native children in the southwestern United States who have been labeled retarded have failed in the white school systems because their culture teaches them that it is wrong to compete in any way. These examples show us that many children who crowd our special classes for the mentally retarded may not actually be retarded.

Parenting and its problems

The parents of the slow child have a very difficult job. Their child experiences a great deal of frustration in trying to learn and function in everyday situations. The parents also have to deal with their feelings of disappointment and their concern for the child's future. In cases of extreme retardation, they have to decide whether to try to deal with the child at home or place him in a special hospital or institution. Today there is a great emphasis on the value of home care. There is no way the personnel in most institutions can give a child the same amount of attention that parents can. On the other hand, caring for the retarded child at home can be difficult and emotionally trying. Parents and other members of the family sometimes feel depressed, exhausted, and at their wits' end. These feelings are normal. There are now many support groups and community organizations that can help parents understand and deal with the stress of raising a mentally retarded child.

When parents first suspect their child has a problem, they should seek more than one professional opinion about the nature of the disability and what it means for the child's future. There have always been people who try to make predictions, when a child is very young, about how much he will be able to accomplish or learn. One mother I knew was told at the moment of her child's birth that the child would never be able to take care of himself or learn anything because he had Down's syndrome. Although it's rare, some Down's children develop to have only slightly lower than average intelligence. Another Down's syndrome child, now in his twenties, outdistanced what the mother — a teacher I once worked with — and her husband expected of him. When the boy was small, they were told he would never be able to leave the house by himself or function on his own. Today he has a job in a sheltered workshop and takes public transportation in a large city without any help. His parents now look to a time when he will be able to live in a group home on his own. His mother believes he might have done even more if she and her husband had realized his potential when he was young. Many mentally retarded children surpass the predictions made about them. This has encouraged many professionals to be more careful about making predictions; still, it's always good to get a second or third opinion and to have the situation evaluated over the years.

There is no doubt that parents and teachers of children who are retarded — and especially those who only function as if they are — can do much with a positive attitude. Although it is not wise to have unrealistic goals or to try to push a child unreasonably, parents sometimes fall into the habit of doing everything for their retarded child or of being overprotective. The child should be given opportunities to do things for himself and learn what he can. The parents must also develop patience and remember that although it is difficult for a retarded child to learn something, it doesn't mean he cannot learn it. I worked with a twenty-year-old man who had just learned to read and print. It took him a long time, but he did it, and he was one of the most determined and good-natured people I have ever met.

Finding the proper placement

Retardation has many degrees. In most schools children are given IQ tests to determine whether they are retarded. Often children whose scores are slightly lower than average are labeled "mildly retarded." But it is quite possible for a child of average or even high intellectual ability to get a very low score on an intelligence test. This is particularly true if the child is suffering from learning disabilities or emotional problems. (This is another reason parents shouldn't settle for just one opinion about their child's difficulties.)

Once parents are satisfied with the diagnosis and evaluation of their child, they can begin to look for the appropriate placement for him in a special school or classroom. Many of the best schools have affectionate, caring teachers who are skilled in using behavior modification and positive reinforcement techniques. Early in my career I saw what a tremendous effect a good teacher could have. As part of my graduate-school training, I worked with a teacher in New Mexico. This woman had been honored across the state for the work she did with children. Each year she was given a class of twelve to fifteen children who had been rejected by other teachers in the Albuquerque school system. Even the special-education teachers had not been able to handle them. Every child had more than one serious disability. The children suffered from combinations of emotional disturbance, mental retardation, hyperactivity, and physical disability. The class was designated for the multiply handicapped.

The teacher structured the class with firm limits and consequences and tempered it with love, appropriate touch, and positive reinforcement. Every September she started out with a group of undisciplined, chaotic children, whose attention spans lasted between five to fifty seconds. By June she had a group of enthusiastic learners who could listen to someone talk for as long as thirty minutes. After one year in this class, about half the children who had been considered without hope re-entered regular classrooms. I will be the first to admit that this particular teacher was a bit of a miracle worker and that we can't expect to see this high a percentage of special education children returning to the regular classroom. But her accomplishments can serve to remind us that hope exists and that an optimistic — if realistic — attitude is better than a pessimistic one.

More effective means of dealing with intellectual deficiency are creating hope for children who once would have been locked in institutions for the rest of their lives. A great deal of responsibility rests on the parents to make sure everything possible is done for their child. And yet the parents need to be as loving, supporting, and patient with themselves as they are willing to be with their child. Skilled, caring professionals exist to help the child with mental retardation — and his parents — along the way.

Chapter Sixteen

The whirlwind child

The terms *hyperactivity* and *learning disabilities* have received quite a bit of media coverage in the last few years. Although many people are familiar with terms, there is widespread misunderstanding of what the terms mean. This lack of understanding can have tragic results when the parents of hyperactive children or children with learning disabilities fail to get help for the children because they don't understand what the problem is. Magazines frequently carry articles about how deeply these children — and their families — suffer. A hyperactive child's incomprehensible behavior can wreak havoc on a marriage and push the parents beyond their limits of tolerance. Some statistics indicate that as many as one out of ten children may suffer from hyperactivity or have learning disabilities. Parents and teachers must learn to spot these children so they can get the help they need. In this chapter, we define both terms. They do *not*, as many people suppose, mean the same thing. Some of the confusion about the terms has come about because the two disorders do sometimes overlap. About twenty-five percent of children diagnosed as having learning disabilities are also hyperactive. Of children who are diagnosed as being primarily hyperactive, we find that as many as eighty-five percent also have learning disabilities. In this chapter we describe some of the signs and symptoms of the two disorders. We go into some detail, since both hyperactivity and learning disabilities have become pervasive.

Hyperactivity and distractibility

A hyperactive child is one who cannot sit still and who seems to be continuously in some sort of motion. In the past decade the term *hyperactive* has been applied loosely to many types of overactive children who might not technically be hyperactive. Overactivity can be caused by a number of things, for instance anxiety. Experts like Dr. Larry Silver, author of *The Misunderstood Child,* believe true hyperactivity has some neurological base. They believe that there may be some sort of imbalance between the part of the brain that stimulates muscles into movement and the part that tells muscles to slow down. There is, as yet, no absolute proof for this theory, but it makes sense.

The whirlwind child

The type of child who is really hyperactive has generally been so from birth. As a newborn, the hyperactive child often squirms, kicks, and rolls around in her crib a great deal. Almost as soon as she learns to walk, she tries to run. As she grows she continues to be a whirlwind of movement. The hyperactive child rarely stops moving during her waking hours. Unfortunately, very little of this movement is productive. I have seen hyperactive children as old as seven or eight accidentally spill their milk, knock their plates off the table and put the jam jar in the butter dish — all in the same meal. The word *accidentally* is a key, for the hyperactive child rarely does these things intentionally. Rather, she seems to be running on a souped-up inner engine that won't slow down long enough for her to do things right. This brings up a second characteristic, which is noticeable at a fairly early age — the seeming clumsiness or lack of coordination of the hyperactive child. All children are somewhat clumsy, and for the hyperactive child it is often hard to say if her continual stumbling, crashing, and dropping is due to a lack of coordination or to the speed with which she is trying to do things.

According to Dr. Larry Silver hyperactive children are also often very distractible. They have trouble concentrating and have short attention spans. Not all distractible children are hyperactive, but a high percentage of distractible children have learning disabilities. Some specialists believe this difficulty is caused by a specific neurological problem in the brain. Fortunately, as many as eighty-five percent of children diagnosed as having hyperactivity or distractibility grow out of the problem around the time of puberty. Many others do so by the time they are young adults. (Parents should note that there is some disagreement about the use of these terms. The American Psychiatric Association considers hyperactivity and distractibility two characteristics of a syndrome they now call Attention-Deficit Hyperactivity Disorder.)

Specific learning disabilities

Learning disability is a term used to label or lump together a certain set of characteristics that have been found to occur in many children who have difficulty in school but who have average or above-average intelligence. A child might have a few of these characteristics, but unless they cause her difficulties in learning or in functioning in general, they are not learning disabilities. A child does not need to have all the characteristics to be headed for the difficulties most children with learning disabilities have.

One way to get a handle on exactly how these specific disabilities interfere with learning is to consider a simplified version of the four steps that have to take place in the brain for learning to occur. These are: input, integration, memory, and output. Many experts believe that specific learning disabilities can occur at any point in this process. This is a rather fancy way of saying that when a child with a learning disability is trying to grasp a piece of information, something seems to go haywire when it's on its way into the child's brain or when she tries to make sense of it, to remember it, or to express it. Problems with processing information may be motor, visual, auditory, or spatial in nature; other problems involve language. None of these difficulties has anything to do with what we think of as a physical disability; in other words, a child with visual learning disabilities has nothing wrong with his eyes or his ability to *see* in the usual sense of the word. These problems occur with schoolwork and with anything in life the child has to learn, understand, or express.

In this chapter we provide an overview of some of the most common and noticeable problems, but parents who suspect they have a hyperactive or learning disabled child might want to read specific books on the subjects (see our Guide to Books on Parenting), and will need to talk to specialists in the field.

Early signs

Only a few characteristics are noticeable before a child begins to read or write. One of these is poor motor coordination. Babies with this problem may have difficulty sucking and eating; they seem to flop around more than other children and are generally more uncoordinated. As we've said, extreme clumsiness can be related to the rushing of a hyperactive child; however, it can also be a specific characteristic of a type of learning disability, which is called *gross motor disability*. This term means the child has trouble coordinating the movements of the gross — or large — muscle groups in the body. The child may stumble and bump into things often; she might also have a hard time with physical activities, like running, jumping, climbing, and swimming.

Another early warning sign is an inability to develop right- or left-handedness. By four or five years of age at the latest, most children have developed a definite preference for using either the right or left hand for activities like eating and coloring. Many children with learning disabilities continually switch from one hand to the other and often begin school without knowing which hand to write with. Although this is not a great problem in itself, it may be indicative of other difficulties that may follow.

Once a child begins to write

Other signs become apparent after a child begins to learn to write. Some of these are related to problems with *fine motor coordination* — the ability to work the small muscle groups, for instance, those in our hands, which we use when we write or do handicrafts. Since the child has difficulty in getting these muscles to work together smoothly, she will have difficulty holding the pencil and getting it to go where she wants. No matter how hard she tries, her printing will usually be messy and illegible.

Another problem that shows up once a child begins to print and read is the inability to to distinguish certain letters from each other. For example, the letters *d, b* and *p* and the letters *g* and *q* are often confused or reversed. Or whole words may be reversed, making *was* into *saw* or vice versa. Almost all children make these mistakes sometimes when they are learning to read and write, but for the child with a learning disability the problem persists. This reversal of letters and words is sometimes called dyslexia. Some people use the term *dyslexia* to refer to any reading problem that is associated with learning disabilities. Others use the term to refer to the inability to learn to read by conventional methods. Because of the confusion surrounding the term, many educators avoid it.

Orientation in space

One of the factors contributing to a tendency to reverse words and letters may be the child's lack of ability to orient herself in space. Children with this learning disability do not seem to have an awareness of where their bodies are in relation to the things around them. This means that some of the things we assume everyone sees in the same way, like the position of something in space, may look different to a child with a learning disability. To illustrate this, you could take the following symbols:

┠ ┙ ㇏ ┝ ┷

and ask a group of young children with learning disabilities to tell you which one looks like a chair they could sit on. Several of the group might have difficulty answering the question correctly.

Order and organization

It is easy to imagine that a child who is racing at top speed with little awareness of how objects around her are placed in space would have a great deal of difficulty putting her environment in order. The task is awesome to a child with learning disabilities, and she will sometimes fall apart when faced with what would seem to us a simple organizing task.

The lack of ability to put things in order or in sequence is another characteristic of a learning disability. A teacher testing to see if a child has this problem might put four colored blocks — red, yellow, blue, green — down in a certain order in front of the child. The teacher would then hand the child four similar blocks, jumbled up, and ask her to put these blocks in the same order. A child who has problems with sequencing will have difficulty doing it. A six- or seven-year-old with learning disabilities might not be able to do it at all, while an eight-year-old might be able to arrange four blocks, but perhaps not six.

How some of these problems relate

Let's use the example of putting blocks in order to see how a teacher or specialist might try to discover whether the child's difficulty with the task lies with input, integration or memory. Say the child is a seven-year-old named Michael who has not yet had any help for his problems. If I wanted to do an informal test with him, I would set out the four blocks and leave them on the table while Michael puts his in the same order. If this task is too easy, I'd add more blocks and make the color patterns more complicated. If Michael has no problem with this task, I know he isn't having problems with visual input, or perception.

Next, I would set down the four colored blocks and let Michael look at them. Then I'd pick mine up and tell him to put his down in the same order. If I discover that Michael can do this with four blocks, but not with five or six, it tells me Michael is probably having problems in his mind integrating — or making sense of — what he sees. Or he might be having a problem with memory. If so, he might be able to remember the order of five blocks after going over it ten or twelve times. If the problem is with integration, memorizing won't help.

What causes learning disabilities

There is a great deal of controversy about what causes learning disabilities. A few theorists claim they have a purely psychological basis. Others feel there may be a number of different physical causes. In some cases, they think that the difficulties may have been caused by what has been called *minimal brain dysfunction*. This is a slight or subtle brain damage that cannot be measured with brain-testing equipment. This minor brain damage may be caused by some difficulty during delivery, a lack of oxygen, toxins, an infection, or high fever. None of this has yet been proven.

Some experts believe heredity is involved. According to some studies, between twenty-five and forty percent of children with learning disabilities have a close relative who has the same problem. Identical twins are both much more likely to have the problem than fraternal twins.

Another theory is that learning disabilities are caused by maturational delay. In other words, the parts of the brain that control visual and auditory perception, memory and so on, may mature more slowly in some children than in others. There is no way to prove this theory, either. Another recent theory is that learning disabilities might be caused by imbalances in brain chemistry. Another idea is that hyperactivity and learning disabilities are caused by allergies or by diets that include high amounts of refined flour and white sugar.

Many experts feel there is probably a physical basis for learning disabilities, but that psychological factors play a role in how they are manifested. No one knows for sure. Most experts agree that there is nothing at all to be gained when parents blame themselves.

Help is available!

If several of the signs we have described are present in a child over a period of time, the parents should seek professional advice and get the child special help if it is needed. In spite of all the talk about learning disabilities, many elementary teachers have not been trained to recognize or deal with them. One of the most hopeful yet frustrating facts about learning disabilities is that they have nothing to do with lack of mental ability. As we stated earlier, children with learning disabilities frequently have average or above- average intelligence. Often the child is able to use her natural intelligence to compensate for her difficulties. But she feels a great deal of extra frustration because her thoughts usually move much more efficiently than her hands or body.

How to help

Hyperactive children and children with learning disabilities seem to do best in a highly structured situation. They need to have very clear limits and consequences, and they are more successful at any activity when it is organized, structured, and planned out for them. Time spent in unstructured games and activities often seems to make their problems appear worse.

Behavior modification techniques can be used to give these children clear goals, and to help them attain them. Positive reinforcement is invaluable, as the self-image of the child with a learning disability is often shattered at an early age. In the case of the hyperactive child, for example, the parent or teacher can praise the child and make positive comments when she does something carefully, moves slowly, spends time quietly, or organizes herself. In particular, the adult needs to compliment any improvements, however small, the child makes in her ability to concentrate or stick with one task.

Another technique for helping these children, especially those who are hyperactive, is to give them opportunities to use their energy in a constructive way. This can range from allowing regular time for physical exercise to using the troubleshooting techniques talked about in Chapter Nine. Keep a a careful eye on the child whenever she is involved in a quiet activity, and watch for the point when you think she can no longer contain herself. Just before that point, interrupt her work and ask her to do a small task that involves physical activity. This gives the child an opportunity to let off some steam. If hyperactive children and children with learning disabilities are allowed to build up tension and energy until they explode or jump up in the middle of a task, they have a very hard time coming back to it.

I have seen the effectiveness of this technique in my work with many children, particularly Brian, a twelve-year-old stick of dynamite. He was creative, knowledgeable, intelligent, and eager to do well. He was also hyperactive and plagued with several frustrating learning disabilities. Brian's span of concentration reached a maximum of fifteen minutes. About every twelve to thirteen minutes, I would find him something to do. I would ask him to sharpen a pencil or bring something from the supply closet. Or I would let him stand up and move around as he organized his work space. The time between the brief periods of physical activity was not regulated by the clock but by certain warning signs, such as increased jitteriness and jerky movements.

This kind of troubleshooting gives the child a legitimate channel for her pent-up energy. It can be used like positive reinforcement to help the child develop longer periods of concentration. Brian's fifteen-minute periods of attentiveness had been built up in a few months from a five-minute attention span.

Keep it fun

The kind of attention a child with a learning disability needs can be provided by a special class or clinic or by a special-education teacher. There is also a great deal a parent can do to help. The caution, of course, is that whatever the parent does has to be fun, or at least very pleasant. Any parent who forces the child into extra schoolwork or who tries to help with homework and ends up belittling or criticizing the child is doing more harm than good. For this reason, some experts object to parents helping their children. Dr. Kason and I feel that family members can make a contribution — if they make sure the activities aimed at helping the child are low-key, no-stress, and positive, and if their attitude is patient, loving, and supportive.

Many daily household activities involve skills children with learning disabilities need to develop. Setting the table is one; getting dressed, sorting cutlery, stacking pots and pans, organizing drawers are a few more. Games also provide training. Almost all card games develop at least a few skills. The cards need to be stacked and shuffled, which involve fine motor coordination, and they have to be organized and put in order for some games. Other card games require matching cards or putting things in sequence. All these tasks sharpen important skills.

In their book *Your Child Can Win*, Joan Noyes and Norma MacNeill provide an excellent list of games and activities, and pinpoint the skills these games develop. They also suggest a number of commercial games. In my work, I often used games like Concentration to develop visual memory and Spill and Spell to work on organization. Snakes and Ladders, Bingo, Checkers, Monopoly, Chinese Checkers, and Chess can all help children at different levels develop math and other skills.

Again, the key is the family's attitude. These activities must never be turned into a testing ground for the child. If mistakes and errors have to be pointed out, it should be in a positive and constructive way. When a child is doing her best or trying hard, she should be rewarded, and progress, no matter how small, should be noticed. Games must remain fun; the object of a game, even one that will help a child, is relaxation and enjoyment. Armed with a loving attitude, a family can do a great deal to help a child overcome her difficulties.

Many children with learning disabilities also develop emotional problems and have trouble relating to others. In this chapter we have described only a few of the hindrances these children must deal with every day. No wonder they become angry and frustrated. No wonder these feelings sometimes lead to emotional or psychological problems. It's also easy to see how their disabilities make it difficult for them to fit in and make friends. The child's problems may also create or worsen difficulties within the family. When this happens the child sometimes is forced to live with an extra burden of animosity or guilt. Although a situation might seem hopeless, remember that tremendous strides have been made. Two decades ago learning disabilities went undetected. Today skilled professionals and organizations like the Association for Children with Learning Disabilities can offer assistance.

Chapter Seventeen

Mickey: a disturbed child and the power of love

There are many forms of emotional disturbances in children. They range from mild behavioral problems to acute forms of schizophrenia. Countless theories have been developed to explain the causes of these disturbances. The theories often conflict. Many parents tend to blame themselves and the way they have raised the child when any type of emotional problem arises. Dr. Kason and I think it is a good idea to take a brief look at what the doctors and psychologists think the causes might be.

Some theorists believe mental illnesses are caused by organic factors; in other words, the causes are physical rather than psychological or emotional. Heredity, vitamin deficiencies, allergies, improper diet, imbalances in brain chemistry, and glandular malfunctions have all been cited as possible organic causes of emotional disturbances in children.

Others think childhood mental illness is caused by some difficulty in the child's environment. Within this broad concept are many different and conflicting theories, but most of these theorists look to the child's home life to find the cause of his emotional disturbance. They look to see if he has suffered from a lack of love, touch, or attention. They explore the child's history to see if it includes a broken home, child abuse, or parents who are unhappily married or who suffer from emotional problems.

Today many experts think that both organic and environmental factors play a role. Some types of mental illness may be caused solely by organic factors, while others may have completely environmental origins. It is suspected, however, that often both factors are involved in one illness. In other words, for some physical reason the possibility of developing a mental illness exists; then environmental factors come into play and influence how severe the problem becomes or whether it even develops at all.

The case of Mickey

Rather than expounding on any one type of childhood mental illness or the theories about the corresponding treatment, I would like to relate the story of the severely disturbed child named Mickey. I worked with Mickey in a clinical school setting for over a year and a half. This is the story of the first few months. It paints a picture of some of the hardships a disturbed child suffers, some of the ways in which he reacts, and some of his characteristics. Since it is only a short discussion about one child, it can do nothing more than give a brief overview of one type of disturbance. However, it is a beautiful story and it says a great deal about the power of love.

Mickey was seven years old when he came to the special school where I worked, a large, comfortable Victorian house specially designed for severely disturbed children who could not cope with home or the regular school system, but who, for a variety of reasons, were not recommended for residential treatment. The children worked with teachers in the school and were seen by therapists.

Mickey had been diagnosed as autistic, a term that designates a severe type of childhood schizophrenia. An autistic child does not meaningfully communicate or relate to other human beings. It became apparent to us after some time that Mickey was almost certainly not autistic, but placing the correct psychological label on him was not our priority. Our priority was helping him to learn to relate to us, because at seven years of age Mickey had never really "spoken" to anyone. This did not mean that he couldn't talk. He was fluent. However, his speech consisted mainly of vain repetition. He repeated things he heard on television or things he read in the television guide. He would do this for hours on end, revealing an almost perfect memory.

I was assigned to work with Mickey and one other child, Tim, for the school year. At the beginning of September, Mickey's repetitious speech seemed to be senseless, but after some time it began to take on meaning. We began to decipher a code that Mickey was using to communicate. He would tell me that he was feeling good or was in agreement with something I suggested by saying the name of a television show he liked. Shouts of "Barney Miller" throughout the school meant that Mickey was having a good day. He expressed his negative feelings and his rejection of suggestions by using this "television language" to block out the people around him. At these times he would sit, sometimes literally for hours, and recite the television guides he had committed to memory.

Mickey used his television language to communicate by repeating commercials. When he recited a commercial, it meant he wanted what that particular commercial was offering. Because Mickey, like most disturbed children, was extremely intuitive, he picked up the underlying message behind the commercial, and this, not the actual advertised product, was what he wanted. He once repeated part of a certain commercial for a cold remedy for days. I happened to see it on television one day and noticed that the person who had the cold was being hugged and kissed. I realized that when Mickey repeated this particular commercial, he was calling out for love and physical affection.

There was not a person in the school, staff or child, who was not happy to oblige Mickey in his need for love. He was picked up, hugged, and carried around the school by everyone, even children only slightly bigger than he was.

No ability to deal with frustration

In spite of all the affection he received, Mickey had many hard times. Like most disturbed children, he had no ability to deal with frustration. Even the slightest failure in his schoolwork would bring him to tears, and when he could not make others understand his wants or needs, his crying would escalate into tantrums.

These periods of frustration were often marked by bouts of destructiveness. Mickey's destructiveness was usually aimed at himself, things he had made, or things he was involved in. For instance, he would often play Snakes and Ladders with Tim. Tim, who had a compulsive nature, always insisted the game be played by the rules. But Mickey felt everyone playing the game should only take forward moves. When Mickey would land on a square that would send him sliding down a snake, he would refuse to move. Because Mickey did not communicate with meaningful words, there was no way for him to express how he wanted to play. Mickey's nature was warm, lovable, and generous. He didn't want Tim to move back, either. This would invariably result in a fight between the two boys. As they argued, Mickey's frustration would mount until he would throw the game onto the floor.

The pattern was repeated with his artwork. When he was angry or frustrated, he would often run to the art room and destroy a picture or construction he had labored over. He would then collapse in tears. This kind of behavior is often a disturbed child's way of expressing his dislike for himself.

Hearts went out to Mickey

No matter how many times Mickey's frustrations and rages interrupted activities or caused problems around the school, there was not one child or teacher whose heart did not go out to him. He continually expressed his kindness by sharing what he had with the other children and hugging and kissing the staff. His love was returned tenfold by the other children, and it was undoubtedly this love that cracked the icy barrier that prevented Mickey from using real words to communicate.

One twelve-year-old child, Peggy, was particularly fond of Mickey. She carried him when he was sad, hugged him when he needed affection, and was his intuitive interpreter in arguments. Probably more than any psychologist, social worker, or teacher who was involved with Mickey, she led to his first meaningful use of language.

The day stands out clearly in my memory. Christmas vacation was nearing. It was a frightening time for many of the children who had begun at the school in September. Several of the children came from violent and abusive homes, and during the vacation they would have to face two solid weeks without the love, security, and support they received daily at the school. This created an atmosphere of tension when the children gathered in the common room for their Christmas party. Many of the faces were solemn, and several fights broke out. Just as things had settled down and the children began to sing the last carol before leaving for home, Mickey crawled onto Peggy's lap. He put his arms around her and said the first meaningful words we had ever heard him speak — "I love you, Peggy."

The power of love

Dr. Kason and I believe that love can be a powerful positive force. Several of the psychologists and teachers at the school believed that their work had probably not had the same impact on Mickey that Peggy's persistent love and affection had. Of course, to say the clinical therapy and treatment Mickey received at school had not had an effect would not be true. The setting, the attitude of the teachers, therapists, and students, the consistent discipline and the skill of the school's director — all these things were important in creating the kind of atmosphere in which Mickey would feel safe enough to begin to open up.

There is no doubt that we have much to learn about childhood mental illness. It may well be that science will find evidence that biological and genetic factors, nutrition, and other physical determinants are involved in the cause of emotional disturbances in children. However, we are convinced that the role of physical affection, common sense discipline, and plain old-fashioned love will continue to play a tremendous part in the prevention of childhood mental illness and in its cure.

Chapter Eighteen

Conclusion: Hug me, hold me, tell me I'm good

We would like to emphasize two points we mentioned in the preceding chapters. Both of them have to do with a child's image of herself and her feelings of self-worth. The first is related to the tremendous importance of *touch*. Children need desperately to be held, cuddled, kissed, and rubbed. Just how desperately they need this may come as a shock to many people. Many years ago it was common for infants who were placed in orphanages or other institutions to die before they reached one year of age. The disease was called *marasmus*, which meant, literally, "wasting away." The interesting fact about the disease was that there was no known physical cause for it. The infants were all receiving adequate food, clothing, and shelter, and they suffered from no obvious illnesses.

Even as late as the 1920s and 1930s, infantile death plagued institutions for foundlings. Ashley Montague, in his book *Touching — The Human Significance of the Skin*, quotes doctors from that era who reported death rates of a hundred percent for infants who spent a major portion of their infancy in these institutions. The situation was so grim that at one institution in New York City the word "hopeless" was used to describe the condition of every infant who was admitted. Some progress was made by the late 1920s, when a few eminent doctors began to realize the one thing the babies were not getting in institutions that they would have gotten in their own homes was a great deal of caressing and cuddling.

Some doctors instigated "mothering" programs in their institutions, in which volunteers would hold and caress the babies several times a day. While these institutions had remarkable success with their programs, it was not until after World War Two that the importance of touching became recognized. Situations during the war prompted studies on marasmus, and it was found to be a significant factor in deaths not only in institutions but also in good homes. The babies in both situations were being deprived of physical affection. The well-educated mothers of the day — from 1900 to 1930 — were influenced by Luther Emmett Holt, a famous pediatrician. Holt was the first advocate of the idea that picking babies up and holding them would spoil them. He went so far as to tell mothers their instinctive cuddling and caressing was a vicious and harmful act.

The upper-class mothers were the ones who came in contact with these teachings. In their efforts to do the right thing they followed his advice. Their babies became emotionally starved, or died. Lower-class mothers, who had never been exposed to Holt's ideas, lavished affection on their babies. These children as a whole, continued to thrive. While childhood deaths did, of course, occur they were not generally from marasmus.

Out of this experience and others like it came the realization that physical stimulation was as important for survival as food and shelter. While it may be difficult for some people to accept the idea that touch is necessary for survival, it should not be difficult for anyone to accept the fact that it is essential for psychological well-being. This idea is virtually undisputed by mental health-care professionals today.

It is important, before we go on, to avoid any possible confusion by making one thing perfectly clear. There is no relationship at all between marasmus and Sudden Infant Death Syndrome which has come to be known as SIDS. It is not yet known what causes SIDS, but it is certainly not lack of touch or stimulation.

Feeling good about touching

Unfortunately, we live in a touch-starved society. North Americans in general tend to feel uncomfortable about touching. It's almost as if we think there is something not quite right about it. The act of touching seems to be acceptable only when there is a *reason* for it: quickly hugging an acquaintance as a greeting, scrubbing a child in the bath, brushing lint off someone's clothes. The only time touching is considered completely acceptable is during sex. And even then some people feel uncomfortable about it.

These feelings vary greatly, of course, from individual to individual. But in our society, touching for the sake of having warm physical contact is rare. This attitude is reflected in the things we teach our children about touching and in the way we touch our children. Someone who is uncomfortable about the act of touching is not going to cuddle a baby as much as someone who feels very good about touching and being touched.

Most babies receive enough touching to survive in the daily process of being cared for and cleaned. Almost all mentally healthy adults find babies lovable and huggable and are naturally drawn to picking up and holding them. Whether children who have reached the age where they can care for themselves receive adequate amounts of hugging and cuddling is a different matter. Thankfully, many do. Others are not so lucky. There is evidence that children who are not touched enough may suffer from varying degrees of psychological difficulties. Some may grow up to be the kind of people who are considered cold, others may have difficulty in forming relationships or expressing themselves sexually; still others may suffer from extreme forms of mental illness. One thing is fairly certain — these people will pass on their distorted feelings about touching to their children.

We should also consider the idea that if touch is this important, children might, in desperation, do anything to get it. One theory we have already mentioned is that children need physical contact so badly that they prefer getting spanked or beaten to not getting any physical contact at all. This means a child who is not receiving enough physical affection may escalate his bad behavior to the point where he is continually being spanked. The disturbed child who lives in a very unhealthy environment may provoke his unstable parents into battering him severely.

How children respond

Children respond in many different ways to their need for physical affection. Some children lap up increased affection; others do not. A parent who suddenly decides she hasn't been hugging her child enough and starts lavishing affection on him may find that the child responds by jerking away and fidgeting. It is possible that the child is uncomfortable with being touched because of unresolved emotional conflicts. Or maybe the child is saying the parent is pouring on too much at once — not that he doesn't want to be touched at all. Remember that a child has picked up many of his parents' attitudes by the time he is around four years of age. At a very early age he may have received the subconscious message that the parent thinks touching is taboo. A sudden change in a parent's attitude may be a shock to him.

When parents want to increase the amount of physical affection they are giving a child, it may be a good idea to proceed slowly, to let a child gradually get used to receiving more hugs. At some point, children begin to think getting hugged is "kid stuff." This doesn't mean that we stop giving physical affection, but our affection takes different forms. Even the most rough-and-tumble preadolescent boy will probably still want that good-night hug and kiss. We can also change the cuddling hugs we give young children into the warm arm around the shoulder, affectionate hugs at emotional moments, and massages for sore muscles.

People who work with children encounter many of the same reactions. In my work with young children I have found that some express their need for physical affection without hesitation; when given the opportunity, they want to be picked up and held. Others shy away from touching and cannot even tolerate a hand on the shoulder. Such children need time to adjust to the adult's warmth and her way of showing it. I have worked with many touch-shy children. Billy was one of these. He could not stand anyone even accidentally brushing against him. When I first began to work with him I refrained from touching him at all. After a time I began to give him an extremely quick pat on the arm. Slowly I increased the amount of time I would rest my hand on his arm. Then I began to put my hand on his shoulder when we worked together. After several months Billy responded happily to an arm placed around his shoulder at appropriate times. Interestingly, as Billy became more accustomed to being touched and to touching, he became far less aggressive in his behavior to other children. While other factors were involved, it may have been that much of the slapping and fighting Billy did was his way of getting the physical contact he so desperately needed.

Our skin — like our eyes and ears — is an organ through which we gather information and perceive things about the world. Billy had learning disabilities and was hyperactive. Overreaction and sensitivity to touch is not uncommon among such children, as messages coming through the skin sometimes get scrambled just as information that comes through their other sensory organs does.

Unless our touch reflects sincere affection, it is of very little use. When we really care about the children we live and work with and show it with appropriate physical warmth, the children will learn to have a positive response to being touched.

Unfortunately, we cannot conclude this section without mentioning a great blight on our society: the rise in the sexual abuse of children. Dr. Kason and I believe that it is imperative we begin teaching children the difference between appropriate and inappropriate touching as soon as they are old enough to understand. Excellent books exist that show you how to do this. Some social-work agencies and local governments have experts who will visit schools and day-care centres and put on presentations that show children how they can learn to tell the difference between appropriate and inappropriate touching. All this is excellent, but in the final analysis it is not enough. Children must have enough confidence in themselves to be able to talk about any adult behavior they find distressing, and they must have enough faith in their parents and teachers to know that they will listen and respect what the children say. Many children sense that what is happening to them is wrong, but they are too afraid to tell.

I am...you are

Appropriate physical affection is one of the ways we teach children how much we care about them and how valuable they are as individuals. One other way we teach children about their self-worth is with the words "You are..." As we have tried to explain, a child builds his self-image to a great extent from what others, particularly his parents, close relatives, and teachers, say about him. The words, "You are..." translate into, "I am..." The child tends to live out the patterns he is taught. A child who hears, "You are clumsy," "You are stupid," "You are bad," "You are an idiot," "You are ugly," incorporates these concepts into his image of himself. Because he has tremendous faith in his parents and teachers, he *believes* the things they say about him with his heart and soul. When he hears particular phrases often enough, they become second nature to him — they *are* him in his own eyes. It does not matter if these things are said in jest or in an attempt to motivate him to do better, it does not even matter if they are in any way true. They *become* true to the child, and he begins to act accordingly.

An increasing amount of evidence supports this theory. The first study done on the subject that attracted international attention was carried out by Robert Rosenthal and Lenore Jacobson in 1964. The two scientists intentionally made up a test that had little or no relevance at all and gave it an impressive name, *The Test of Inflected Acquisition*. They gave the test to an entire grade level in an elementary school. Everyone was given the impression that this was an extremely significant test, and that the results could mean a great deal for the students' futures.

After the students finished taking the test, Rosenthal and Jacobs took the papers away for grading. Teachers and students assumed the tests were being scored in the usual way. The two scientists, however, simply picked five of the students' names at random and assigned the highest grades to them. They returned to the school and told the teachers that these five children's grades were so very outstanding they could be expected to make tremendous gains during the next year.

Amazingly enough, these five students did indeed progress far beyond what previously would have been expected of them during the next school year. They also showed increases in their scores on an IQ test! This was a stunning development, because many educators and psychologists think of an IQ score as something that doesn't change.

Studies like this serve to underline the amazing power our ideas about ourselves have over our performance. Over the years I have worked with countless children whose worst academic problem was a terrible self-image. I have seen boys who could memorize a complicated football play in the blink of an eye or take apart and reassemble a car engine but who, when faced with a page of simple reading, would say, "I can't do that, I am stupid."

I can't do that. I am stupid, I am clumsy. I am ugly. I am bad. I am good for nothing. Our children learn these ideas about themselves from *us* — their parents, teachers, and day-care workers. Quite often adults tell children these things because they think it will help the children do better. The father of one troubled boy I worked with told me, "I tell him he's stupid so he'll try harder." A mother said about her slightly overweight daughter, "I tell her she's fat so she'll lose a little weight." And all of us have, countless times, heard parents say, "You are a bad girl!" to a child whose behavior they want to improve. This kind of statement boomerangs. The "stupid" boy fails, the "fat" child eats, and the "bad" girl gets worse.

Dr. Kason and I believe that, as adults, one of our prime responsibilities is to pay careful attention to the words we use with our children. It should be clear by now that we don't mean people should be insincere. But we should do our best to emphasize the child's positive characteristics and strengths. We can build a child up in his own mind without inflating his ego. It is just as easy for him to learn "I am smart," "I am kind," "I am good," "I am healthy," as it is for him to learn that he is dumb or bad. Neither of us would speak with such deep conviction on this principle if we had not personally seen it work many times.

At the beginning of this book we said our purpose was to help you develop an attitude for dealing with the children you live and work with. This attitude is based on looking for the best in our children. Not to lie or to tell them things we don't mean, but to look for and expect the best. This is also true about ourselves as parents and teachers. We need to have confidence in ourselves, to learn to do things that make us feel good about ourselves, and to be sure we get the warmth and affection *we* need as individuals.

Dr. Kason and I have worked with children so tragically disturbed that they have tried to kill themselves and others, children who were so profoundly schizophrenic they could not tell a friendly gesture from a violent attack. We have worked with the severely retarded, the hyperactive, and the normal child. But we have *never* worked with a child who did not respond in some degree to firm, consistent discipline, warm affection, and love. We have never met a child who didn't want to hear that he was good, who didn't want to hear about the things he did well. We haven't met this child — and we're sure he doesn't exist.

If, as parents, teachers, and day-care workers, we trust ourselves, we can be firm. If we trust our own judgment we can be consistent. If we feel in our hearts a child's need for love, praise, and the warmth of physical affection, we can give it. And our children will respond.

Part Three

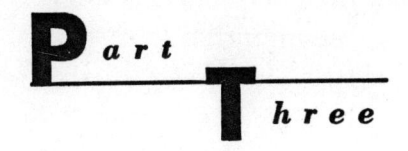

Further reading

Chapter Nineteen

A guide to books on parenting

Few things are more bewildering for parents than a trip to the parenting section in a large bookstore. These sections have become huge. In some large cities whole bookstores are dedicated to books on parenting and child development.

There are hundreds of different books on these subjects, and many of them offer conflicting advice. Parents often become confused and frustrated when they are trying to find the answer to a specific question or to get information on child rearing in general. However, the situation is not as perplexing as it seems. Most of the popular parenting books can be divided into four categories. There are books by Adlerians, behaviorists, and developmentalists, and there are books on child care. A few authors, like Dr. Kason and myself, combine ideas from more than one school of thought. One of the reasons the four categories are not readily apparent to the reader is that many authors promote their ideas without first explaining their philosophical roots. We help clarify this situation by providing brief descriptions of the main schools of thought in parenting, then listing a few of the popular books from each.

Frequently, a school of thought has developed out of the teachings of one person. The founder's original ideas evolve and develop over the years as the founder grows older and his or her students carry on the tradition. Thus, any one school can come to include a wide range of theories and ideas. Our purpose here is to provide you with an overview.

The Adlerians

Alfred Adler was an Austrian psychiatrist who lived from 1870 to 1933. Although he was originally a student of Sigmund Freud's, Adler eventually came to disagree with Freud on a number of points and finally broke away from him in 1911. A great deal of Adler's work centered on the feelings of inferiority people have and the difficulties these feelings cause. He was also concerned with the proper rearing and education of children. In 1921 he opened the first child-guidance clinic in Vienna, Austria. Later, he moved to the United States and continued his work, always emphasizing the importance of sound child guidance.

A guide to books on parenting

Many Adlerian psychologists have concentrated their efforts on child psychology and on how Adler's ideas apply to the relationship between parent and child. Although current Adlerians differ somewhat in their individual approaches, they generally all believe in the following principles of child rearing:

- ❏ The family should be a democracy. Each member of the family has an equal claim to dignity and respect. Parents don't rule over children; men don't rule over women. Each person has a vote in family decisions.

- ❏ Ideally, the goal in child rearing is for children to *learn* to behave properly from the consequences of their behavior rather than from their parents telling them what to do. Spanking is not acceptable.

- ❏ Most Adlerians recommend the family meeting or council, in which adults and children work together, or brain-storm in order to find solutions to problems.

- ❏ Encouraging cooperation between parents and children is a goal — it makes it easier for children to learn acceptable behavior. An atmosphere of mutual respect is essential.

- ❏ Parents are encouraged to use "I messages" — statements that express the adult's feelings but do not criticize or judge the child. Children should be treated in a manner that fosters self-esteem.

The Adlerians whose books about parenting are most popular today are Rudolf Dreikurs and Thomas Gordon, the founder of Parent Effectiveness Training, and Haim Ginnot and two of his followers, Adele Faber and Elaine Mazlish.

Adlerian books

Children: the Challenge. Rudolf Dreikurs and Vicki Soltz, Hawthorn Press, 1964. One of the classic books on discipline from the Adlerian perspective. It is rather long and fairly intellectual, but it is still useful. This is a good background text for a parent who enjoys reading. He is firmly against spanking. We are not comfortable with his extreme position on natural consequences.

Between Parent and Child, Haim Ginnot, Avon Books, 1956. Reprinted 1969. Another classic Adlerian book. It emphasizes the importance of understanding the messages children sometimes send with their behavior. It focuses on children from six to ten.

Between Parent and Teenager, Haim Ginnot, Avon Books, 1971. Similar to *Between Parent and Child*, but with a focus on teenagers.

How To Talk So Kids Will Listen And Listen So Kids Will Talk, Adele Faber and Elaine Mazlish, Avon Books, 1980. An excellent book on communication and discipline. Based on Haim Ginnot's teachings, it is clearly written, humorous and easy to read. It emphasizes engaging a child's cooperation and is against spanking. Good examples of how to use active listening are provided. Well worth reading if you want more information on the Adlerian approach.

Siblings Without Rivalry, Adele Faber and Elaine Mazlish, Avon Books, 1988. Humorous and easy to read, this book applies the Adlerian philosophy to raising siblings in an atmosphere that lessens rivalry by promoting dignity and mutual respect.

Parent Effectiveness Training, Thomas Gordon, New American Library, 1975. A readable book, it stresses the use of "I messages" and active listening for dealing with behavior problems. Gordon is against spanking. The book provides many useful insights.

P.E.T. in Action, Thomas Gordon, Wynden Books, 1976. In this book Gordon reviews the successes and failures parents have had using parent effectiveness training in the home. In order to benefit from the information you need to first read *Parent Effectiveness Training*.

The Parents Handbook — STEP — Systematic Training For Effective Parenting, Don Dinkmeyer and Gary McKay, American Guidance Service, 1982. Easy to read, full of pictures, charts and diagrams. This book promotes the ideas of Rudolf Dreikurs.

Behavior modification

Behavior modification is a technique that has grown out of a field called behavioral psychology. The behaviorism school was founded by a psychologist named John B. Watson in the early 1900s. Watson was influenced by the work of the Russian scientist Ivan Pavlov, who was famous for his experiments that showed how a dog's responses could be conditioned by rewards. The most famous behaviorist is probably B.F. Skinner, a psychologist who developed the concepts of programmed learning and teaching machines. In the classroom, a child using a programmed learning workbook or teaching machine works alone and learns at his or her own pace by being rewarded immediately for correct answers.

Behavioral psychologists are concerned with correcting specific, unwanted behavior rather than resolving underlying psychological causes. One of the best things that can be said for behavioral techniques is that they often work quickly. Psychologists who are not behaviorists — called in general cognitive theorists — tend to think of behavior modification as a kind of Band-Aid technique that may get rid of a negative behavior but that does not solve the problem that caused it in the first place. Many good techniques have originated from work done by behaviorists. These include the use of positive reinforcement, time outs, behavior modification charts, and contracts. A few of the basic behaviorist ideas that relate to child rearing are:

- ❑ All behavior is learned.
- ❑ When a child has learned an inappropriate behavior, he or she can learn an appropriate behavior to replace it.

A guide to books on parenting

- ❑ We can teach children how we want them to behave through the use of positive reinforcers like praise, stickers and treats — or through the use of negative reinforcers like punishment.
- ❑ The most effective negative reinforcer is one that, like a time out, gives the child as little attention as possible.

Gerald Patterson and Howard Sloane are two behaviorists whose books are now popular.

Behavior modification books

Families: Applications of Social Learning to Family Life, Gerald R. Patterson, Research Press, 1975. A comprehensive yet readable book. Focuses on positive reinforcement, contracts, time out and behavioral reward charts. Like many behaviorists, Patterson stresses the use of positive rewards and punishment to change behavior. We prefer an approach that places more emphasis on the positive reinforcement of desired behavior than on the punishment of undesirable behavior.

Living with Children: New Methods for Parents and Teachers, Gerald R. Patterson and M. Elizabeth Gullion, Research Press, 1968. Revised 1976. This book deals with behavioral reward charting and time out. Although some of the approaches may be useful, the format of the book, which is written as a programmed learning text, is a distraction. We are not comfortable with the authors' suggestion to put children in the bathroom for their time outs.

The Good Kid Book: How to Solve 16 Most Common Behavior Problems, Howard N. Sloane, Research Press, 1988. This book focuses on specific problematic behavior. Techniques used are positive reinforcement, behavioral reward charting, and the shaping of behavior.

Discipline Without Shouting or Spanking, Jerry Wyckoff and Barbara Unell, Meadowbrook Books, 1984. A short book, and easy to read. The subject matter is broken down according to the specific behavior you wish to change. Simple behavioral approaches are based on positive reinforcement and the use of time out.

Don't Shoot the Dog: The New Art of Teaching and Training, Karen Pryor, Bantam Books, 1984. Short and clearly written, this book focuses on the use of positive reinforcement and on how to shape behavior. An interesting book.

Developmentalists

Many books on parenting don't deal with the question of discipline at all. They focus instead on the different developmental stages that children go through as they grow. Such books are generally written by psychiatrists or psychologists who can be called, in this context, developmentalists. They provide information on the physical and mental abilities — or the skills — a child should have mastered at any particular age. Some developmentalists also deal with the types of behavior that go along with certain stages.

It's generally helpful for parents to have at least one book that outlines the stages of child development. The caution is that it is very difficult to say what "normal" or "average" is when it comes to the way individual children grow and learn. Some children reach the stages outlined by the developmentalists much earlier than expected, others much later. A child who is way ahead of schedule is not necessarily going to be exceptionally intelligent, and a child who lags behind is not necessarily going to have a problem with learning later on. In fact, many very intelligent people are slow maturers. Parents can use the developmental stages as guidelines, but should not be concerned if their child doesn't master skills at a certain time. Parents should point out any concerns about their child's development to their pediatrician or family doctor.

Piaget and Gesell

The Swiss psychologist Jean Piaget was the first person to make a really systematic study of the way children acquire their ability to understand and learn. Piaget lived from 1896 to 1980, and he is thought by many to be the major figure in developmental psychology. He found that the development of a child's ability to think proceeded according to a timetable set down by nature. Further, it was simply not possible to teach a child a particular concept or get the child to think in a certain way until the child's mind was ready for it. Piaget had a great influence on the attitudes of some educators; he believed that a teacher should not try to pour information into a child's head, but rather should guide a child on a journey of discovery.

Arnold Gesell was born in the United States in 1880. Gesell, who had doctorates in psychology and medicine, launched his first major study on child development in 1926. Gesell's studies were concerned with physical and mental development. One of his main points was that children had to reach specific stages in maturation before what they learned could begin to effect how they behaved. In child rearing, Gesell promoted what he called *discerning guidance* which was opposed to the two extremes popular at the time, rigid authoritarianism and excessive permissiveness. Much of what we understand today about developmental behavior has come from the work done at the Gesell Institute. Two popular authors from the institute are Frances Ilg and Louise Ames.

The Freudians

Several people who write books on child development have a Freudian background. They are not developmentalists in the same sense as Gesell and Piaget. Freud was the founder of psychoanalysis and the person who first showed us that each of us has a conscious and a subconscious mind. Freud believed that the mental and emotional problems of adults began in childhood. Those who write on child development from a Freudian perspective tend to focus on the development of the child's mind and personality as he or she goes through the various stages Freud outlined, rather than on the development of skills. Two well-known writers from this field are Selma Fraiberg and Bruno Bettelheim.

Books on development

Infant and Child in the Culture of Today, Arnold Gesell, Frances Ilg, and Louise Ames, Harper and Row, 1974. This book presents the usual development and developmental behavior of a child from birth to five years of age. Like other books written by authors from the Gesell Institute, this book does not deal with the question of discipline in any detail.

Your One-Year-Old, Louise Ames and Frances Ilg, Delacorte, 1982. This book focuses on the developmental behavior of the one-year-old child. Ames and Ilg have a series of books on specific ages, including *Your Two-Year-Old*, *Your Three-Year-Old*, *Your Four-Year-Old*, and *Your Five-Year-Old*.

The Magic Years, Selma Fraiberg, Scribners, 1959. A Freudian view of child development. Although some sections are good, we disagree strongly with Fraiberg's view on conditional love. Fraiberg advocates withdrawing love from children when they misbehave.

A Good Enough Parent, Bruno Bettelheim, Vintage Press, 1987. Another look at child development from a basically Freudian perspective. Bettelheim's love for children and his sensitivity to their feelings is apparent.

The First Three Years of Life, Burton L. White, Prentice-Hall, 1975, revised, 1987. A detailed examination of a child's physical, emotional, social, and intellectual development from birth to age three. White outlines recommended child rearing practices, toys, and activities to help promote healthy development at each stage.

The First Twelve Months, Frank Caplan, Bantam Books, 1971. Caplan has some interesting ideas, but he sets out a rather rigid time frame for developmental behavior. This may cause parents to worry needlessly. He has written a follow-up called *The Second Twelve Months.*

Infants and Mothers, T. Berry Brazelton, Delacorte, 1969. An interesting book. Brazelton groups babies into the quiet baby, the average baby, and the active baby, and compares thesthree types of babies as they grow.

The Rogerian influence

The Rogerian school of psychology was founded by Carl Rogers, a professor at the University of Chicago from 1945 to 1957. Rogers originated something called *nondirective therapy,* a type of counseling that emphasizes the person-to-person relationship between the therapist and the patient. Rogers called the patient a client. The Rogerian approach is based, in part, on clients' ability to work through their problems for themselves. One of the keys to this process is that therapists must have a totally accepting and nonjudgmental attitude toward the people they are working with. This attitude is sometimes called *positive regard* or *unconditional warm regard*. Another of Rogers's major contributions to the field of psychology was the concept of the empathic response. In the empathic response, the therapist listens to what the client says with great attention, then responds in a way that shows the client the therapist has heard what was said and accepts it without criticism or judgment.

Rogers's methods of nondirective therapy were adapted to children through the use of a technique called play therapy. This revolutionary concept showed how children could work out emotional and psychological problems using toys in a therapeutic setting. Virginia Axline, a student of Rogers', further developed his ideas on play therapy and has long been considered the authority on the subject.

The concepts of unconditional love, nonjudgmental acceptance and the empathic response — regardless of what they are called — are becoming increasingly well-known. Most of the books that promote the Rogerian philosophy are about psychology and not about parenting. However, Rogers' ideas have influenced many people who work with and write about children.

Rogerian books

Dibs in Search of Self, Virginia Axline, Ballantine Books, 1964. A moving story that describes how unconditional love helped cure an emotionally disturbed boy.

Play Therapy, Virginia Axline, Ballantine Books, revised 1981. Although this book has been written for therapists, it is easy to understand, and some parents might be interested in seeing how effective Rogerian techniques can be.

Productive Parenting Skills, Robert Carkhuff, Human Resources Development Press, 1985. Carkhuff was a student of Carl Rogers. This book demonstrates how to apply Rogerian principles to parenting.

Combining different approaches

In *Love, Limits, and Consequences*, Dr. Kason and I take what is known, in psychology, as a cognitive-behavioral approach. We have drawn on the ideas of the cognitive theorists, particularly Rogers, in the development of our overall attitude toward children that stresses acceptance and unconditional love. But we also use techniques such as positive reinforcement that have their roots in behavioral psychology. This combined approach allows us to incorporate all the techniques we have found to be effective into our overall philosophy of child rearing. A few other authors who combine ideas from different schools — although differently than we do — are listed here.

Books that combine theories

How to Parent, Fitzhugh Dodson, New American Library, Signet Press, 1970. Clearly written and easy to read. Most of the book focuses on child development. Two chapters present an approach to discipline based on a combination of ideas from cognitive theorists, such as Carl Rogers, and behavior modification theory. Dodson finds spanking acceptable in certain extreme situations.

How to Discipline With Love, Fitzhugh Dodson, New American Library, Signet Press, 1977. An elaboration on his earlier book. Most of the book consists of frequently asked questions and Dodson's answers. The questions are organized according to the age of the child.

Without Spanking or Spoiling, Elizabeth Crary, Parenting Press, 1979. The book is based on parent effectiveness training, on behavior modification, and on the work of Rudolf Dreikurs, an Adlerian. The material is presented in workbook form, with many charts, tables and exercises. Although the book is informative, the format is distracting.

Child care

There are a number of books that are general handbooks on child rearing, many of them written by doctors. These books discuss everything from feeding schedules to what to do about colic. We think the best one available today is *Dr. Mom* by Marianne Neifert, a pediatrician and mother of five. Every home library needs one good book on basic child care.

Books on child care

Dr. Mom, Marianne Neifert, with Anne Price and Nancy Dana, Signet Books, 1986. This is an excellent handbook for parents. It covers all the basics of child care and raising children. Neifert gives practical advice on most common concerns. There are excellent sections on street proofing, baby proofing your home, toilet training, eating problems, and childhood illness. We recommend this book highly.

A New Life, Pregnancy, Birth, and Your Child's First Year, John T. Queenan with Carrie Neher Queenan, Stoddart Publishing, 1986. A lovely, clearly written book with lots of pictures and diagrams. The authors deal with pregnancy, the preparation for parenthood and adjusting to a new baby in the home, in addition to basic child care. A good book for expecting and new parents.

Babyhood, Penelope Leach, Penguin Books, 1974, revised 1983. One of several books by this author dealing with the care of the newborn and the child to age five. Parts of this book are excellent, but some of Leach's advice on infant feeding is no longer appropriate. Parents will probably find her advice on most common problems useful.

Dr. Spock's Baby and Child Care, Benjamin Spock and Michael Rothenberg, Pocket Books, 1945, revised 1985. This is the classic book on child care. Much of the information still makes very good sense. The book is less readable than *Dr. Mom*, and contemporary issues such as street proofing are not covered.

Books on specific problems

There are books available that focus on one specific behavioral problem, such as bed-wetting or difficulties with bedtimes. These books are usually written from the point of view of one particular school of thought. Thus you can find a variety of books on bed-wetting, some written by cognitive theorists, some by behaviorists. The solutions the authors propose to problems are extremely different.

Several books are also available on more general subjects, such as fathering or single-parenting. These books are often compilations of useful information or relevant personal experiences, and many of them don't promote any one psychological theory.

Sleep problems

Night-time Parenting, William Sears, Plume Books, 1985. A good developmental approach to understanding your child's sleep problems. Sears encourages parents to meet a child's night-time needs for closeness and supports the family-bed concept. An excellent book.

Solve your Child's Sleep Problems, Richard Ferber, Fireside Books, 1985. A modified behavior-modification approach aimed at making children stop disturbing their parents at night. Ferber supports the idea of letting children cry in increasing increments of time. Some parents have found this approach helpful, but we do not generally recommend it.

Single parenting

How to Single Parent, Fitzhugh Dodson, Harper and Row, 1987. This book deals with children's and parents' reactions to divorce or the death of a parent. Dodson discusses the problems of being a single parent, from custody issues to visitation rights to how to come to grips with being single again. A very good book.

Bringing Up Children On Your Own, Liz McNeill Taylor, Fontana Press, 1985. This book deals with all types of single parenthood. It includes comments on being a single parent by choice, on lesbianism, on divorce and on the death of a parent.

Successful Single Parenting, Anne Wayman, Meadowbrook Press, 1987. A very easy-to-read and straightforward guide for the parent who is adjusting to divorce and coming to grips with being single again.

The grieving child

Helping Children Cope with Separation and Loss, Claudia L. Jewett, Harvard Common Press, 1982. This sensitive book covers how children deal with the loss of a parent through divorce, death, absence, adoption, or foster care. Jewett discusses the stages of grief and gives advice on ways to help kids deal with their feelings at each stage. Excellent.

I Don't Know What To Say, Robert Buckman, Key Porter Books, 1988. This is an excellent book about how to talk to and help a person who is dying. Although it is not a book on parenting, one section of the book deals with children's reactions to the loss of a parent or sibling.

Learning disabilities

The Misunderstood Child: A Guide for Parents of Learning Disabled Children, Larry B. Silver, McGraw-Hill Ryerson, 1984. A readable but fairly technical resource book. Silver describes learning disabilities, their psychological and social implications, and diagnosis and treatment. He also discusses hyperactivity.

Smart but Feeling Dumb: The Challenging New Research on Dyslexia and How it May Help You, Harold N. Levinson, Warner Books, 1984. Provides detailed information on dyslexia.

Attention Deficit Disorder: Hyperactivity Revisited, H. Moghadam, Detselig Enterprises, 1988. Moghadam is a Canadian, and the book is very readable. It provides parents with practical information about hyperactivity.

Attention Deficit Disorder and Hyperactivity, Ronald J. Friedman and Guy T. Doyal, Interstate Printers and Publishers, 1987. An excellent overview; more technical than the book by Moghadam.

Your Child Can Win: Strategies, Activities and Games for Parents of Children with Learning Disabilities, Joan Noyes and Norma MacNeill, Macmillan of Canada, 1982. The title of this book describes the book well. Noyes and MacNeill take an extremely positive approach and provide some excellent suggestions for parents. The book is clearly written.

Fathering

Becoming a Father: How to Nurture and Enjoy Your Family, William Sears, La Leche League International, 1986. A sensitive, clearly written book that should inspire fathers to become actively involved in parenting.

The Birth of a Father, Martin Greenberg, Avon Books, 1985. A good book that deals with the adjustments involved in becoming a father and contains a good deal of practical advice.

The Father's Guide to Raising a Healthy Child, Roger M. Barkin, Fulcrum, 1988. An easy-to-read how-to guide. Barkin covers the adjustment to becoming a father, child care, child illnesses, baby proofing and basic discipline.

Learning new parenting habits

I'm OK, You're OK, Thomas A. Harris, Avon Books, 1967. Although this is not a book on parenting or child discipline, Harris's ideas have influenced many parents and teachers. This is the classic book on transactional analysis. The book provides interesting insights into how childhood experiences may affect a person's ability as a parent. Harris' ideas can help people who want to break parenting habits they learned from their parents.

A guide to books on parenting

Born to Win, Muriel James and Dorothy Jongeward, Addison-Wesley, 1971. Another of the classic texts on transactional analysis. The book also provides exercises for the reader based on gestalt psychology. This is not a book on parenting, but it can help parents learn new, more positive ways of relating to their children.

How to Really Love Your Child, Ross Campbell, Signet Press, 1982. An excellent, readable book. Campbell talks about the importance of making sure children feel unconditional love, and tells how to effectively convey love to children. He feels spanking is acceptable only in extreme cases. Written from a Christian perspective, but well worth reading no matter what your ideology.

How to Really Love Your Teenager, Ross Campbell, Signet Press. Campbell applies the ideas in *How to Really Love Your Child* to the special difficulties involved in parenting a teenager.

Each of the major schools of thought on parenting has something to offer. Certain schools will appeal to some people and fit their parenting style more than others. Parents and teachers who are having difficulty dealing with a particular problem might want to read up on a certain school of thought and try out some of the ideas. Each child is an individual, and certain approaches may work better with one child than another. Different situations need to be handled in different ways. All this means that parents and teachers need to have a variety of tools on hand for dealing with — and preventing —

problems. But this does not mean that an adult can simply read a mass of conflicting material on child rearing and then use the methods randomly. You can't expect your discipline methods to work if you are an Adlerian one day and a Rogerian the next, or if you — without sound justification — use behavior modification with one child and reasoning with another.

Any approaches you take to child rearing need to be moulded into a cohesive whole. This is what we have tried to provide for you in *Love, Limits and Consequences*.

Index

Active listening, 182, 183-185
Adlerian psychologists, 124-125, 280-282
Alcohol, 215-216
Alternatives
  for the child, 38, 51, 83-84, 108-110
  to limits and consequences, 40, 114-117
"Anti-argument approach", 203
Anxiety, anticipation, 167-169
Appropriate consequences, 21, 48, 88
Attention
  children's need for, 23, 24, 123
  cries for, 102-103
  failing for, 100-101, 208-210
  negative, 92-93
Autonomy, 201-202
Axline, Virginia, 182, 291

Baby, responding to needs of, 140-142
Bedtime, 169-170
Behavior modification, 90-92, 283-285
  charts, 117-119
  techniques, 117-122
Bettelheim, Bruno, 166
Bragging, 172
Brain damage, 239
Bribery, vs positive reinforcement, 93-94

Cerebral palsy, 239
Child-proofing, 40
Children
  differences among, 126-129
  feelings on the loss of a parent, 225-229
  mentally retarded, 236-246
  perceptiveness of, 54
  a place and things of their own, 110-114, 205
  self-esteem, 125
  as sources of stress, 79-82
  two-year-olds, 199-206
"Choice close", 204-205
Chromosomal abnormalities, 239-240, 243
Clarifying a situation, 168-169, 169-170, 173-174, 176-177
Communication problems, 239, 241-242
Consequences
  appropriate, 21, 48, 88
  fairness of, 56-57
  focus on the misbehavior, not the child, 22, 53-56, 116-117
  following through, 21, 25, 47-48, 52-53, 62
  a framework for good discipline, 83-86
  hints on setting consequences, 87
  inappropriate, 78-79, 89
  logical, 47-48

Consequences (cont.)
  losing privileges, 73-74
  meaning of terms, 45-49
  natural, 46-47
  repairing damage, 74-75
  separation from activity, 67-73
  setting, 49-50
  taking away a toy, 64-65
  time out, 65-66
Consistency of limits, 40-42
Contracting, 119-121
Crying, 181, 192
  babies', 140

Decision making, involving children in, 60
Developmentalists, 286-289
Disruptive behavior, reasons for, 71
Divided families, 223-235
  children's feelings, 225-229
  games separated parents play, 229-233
  role models, 233-235
Divorce, 224-233
Dodson, Dr. Fitzhugh, 182
"Don't", an overused word, 106-108
Down's syndrome, 239-240, 243
Drugs, 215-216
Dyslexia, 252-253

Emotional disturbances, 261-267
  causes, 26, 261-262
Emotions
  accepting versus encouraging, 186-188
  adults, 191
  of children in divided families, 225-229
  clarifying, 185-186, 187-190
  empathic response to help emotional expression, 182-190, 194-195, 219-220, 291
  expressing appropriately, 110-114, 181-182, 192-194, 228-229
  suppressing, 179-181
Empathic response, 182-190, 194-195, 219-220, 291
Expectations
  contracting, 119-121
  explaining to children, 115-117
  reasonable level of, 85-86
Expression
  of emotions, 181-196, 228-229
  providing opportunities for, 110-114, 192-193

Failure for attention, 100-101, 208-210
  other reasons for failure, 214-216
Family problems and school difficulties, 221-222
Fine motor coordination, 252
Following through, 21, 25, 44-45, 52-53, 62
Freudians, 288-289

Games and activities, 259-260, 291
Gesell, Arnold, 288
Gifts, 136-138
  in divided families, 229-230
Gross motor disability, 251-252
Group play, 172-173
Guilt, parental, 26-27

Harris, Dr. Thomas, 158
Holding, 134
Holt, Luther Emmett, 269
Hyperactivity, 247-248, 248-250, 256, 257, 258

"I-messages", 116-117, 191, 192
"In-between times", 166-167, 169-170

Index

Inconsistency, 131, 132-133, 136
Incremental approach, 59-60
Infantilization, 147-148
Insincerity, 138-139

Jacobson, Lenore, 275-276

Lasswell, Marcia, 180, 181
Learning disabilities, 247-248, 250-260
  causes, 255-256
  help for, 256-260
Limits, setting, 28-43
  alternatives to limits, 40, 114-117
  behavior limits, 30-31, 32-33
  consistency of limits, 40-42
  different limits for different kids, 58-60
  different limits for siblings, 37-38
  for hyperactive or learning-disabled children, 256-258
  involving children in setting limits, 60
  limits that fit the child, 36-37
  offering choices to the child, 38, 51, 83-84, 108-110
  other hints, 38-39
  safety limits, 30, 31-32
  saying "don't", 106-108
  setting in advance, 33-34
  and tolerance levels of adults, 34-36
Logical consequences, 47-48
Love
  children's need for love and touching, 136, 138, 139, 141, 142, 268-278
  combining with limits, 17-27
  and a disturbed child, 264, 266-267
  not possessiveness, 144-153
  not spoiling, 131-143
  a positive force, 136, 267
  troubleshooting, see Troubleshooting
  unconditional, 23-24, 54-55

Marasmus, 268-270
Mealtimes, 155-156, 170-171
Memories, recollecting, 156-158
Mental illnesses. See Emotional disturbances
Mental retardation, 236-246
  causes, 238-240
Messes, making, 112-114
Mickey, 262-267
Middle child syndrome, 127-128
Minimal brain dysfunction, 255
Modeling, 114-115
Montague, Ashley, 269

Natural consequences, 46-47
Needs, basic, 122-123
"No Means Yes" approach, 203-204

Order and organization, 253-254
Overprotectiveness, 144-153
  effect on a child's behavior, 146-147

Parents
  learning new parenting habits, 163-164
  overprotective, 144-153
  repeating patterns experienced in childhood, 154-163
  of retarded children, 242-244
Penfield, Wilder, 156-157
Piaget, Jean, 201, 287-288
Play therapy, 291
Positive approach, 22-24, 38. See also Positive reinforcement
  and mentally retarded children, 244, 245-246
Positive reinforcement, 90-105
  around the house, 97-99
  attention is a reward, 92-93
  an example, 94-96
  how to use, 104
  and school, 99-101, 216-219

Positive reinforcement (cont.)
  should be a habit, 96-97
  sincere praise, 101-102
  vs bribery, 93-94
Possessiveness. See Overprotectiveness
Praise, 124-126
  focus on specifics, 125, 126
Prevention of trouble. See Troubleshooting
Private place for kids, 111, 113-114, 205
Privileges, loss of, 73-74
Programming, from childhood, 158
  changing old programming, 159-162
  professional help, 162-163
Punishment, 45-46. See also Consequences

Reminders, 50-51
Repairing damage, 74-75
Rogers, Carl, 54, 182, 290-291
Role models, for children of divided families, 233-235
Rosenthal, Robert, 275-276
Rough behavior, 98-99

School, 207-222
  and family problems, 214-215, 221-222
  and positive reinforcement, 99-101, 216-220
  reasons for failure, 208-216
  special difficulties, 222, 244-246. See also Emotional disturbances; Learning disabilities; Mental retardation

Scolding, 75-76
Self-image, 54, 125, 213-214, 275-277
  combating a poor self-image, 219-220
Sexual abuse of children, 274-275
Shaping a behavior, 98
Siblings, competition with, 210-213
Silver, Dr. Larry, 248, 249
Single-parent families. See Divided families
Skinner, B.F., 90, 284
Spanking, 63-64, 77-78
Spatial orientation, 253
Special education, 245-246
Spoiled children, 131-133
  causes of spoiling, 143-144
Stresses of child rearing, 79-82
Subconscious mind, 157-158

Tantrums, 133-136
Threats, 76-77
Time limits, 38-39
Tolerance levels of adults, and setting limits for children, 34-36
Touching, importance of, 139, 141, 142, 268-278
Treats, 121-122
Troubleshooting, 23, 50, 165-178
  how to troubleshoot, 173-177
  with hyperactive children, 257-258
  using the empathic response to troubleshoot, 190
Two-year-olds, 199-206
  antidotes for the "terrible twos", 203-205